Birgit Nilsson

MY MEMOIRS IN PICTURES

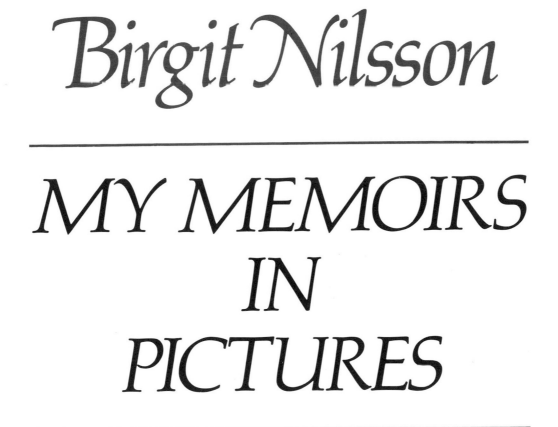

Birgit Nilsson

MY MEMOIRS
IN
PICTURES

Translated from the Swedish by Thomas Teal

DOUBLEDAY & COMPANY, INC., GARDEN CITY, NEW YORK

1981

Originally published in Sweden as *Mina minnesbilder* by Albert Bonniers Förlag in 1977
Library of Congress Cataloging in Publication Data Nilsson, Birgit. My memoirs in
pictures. Translation of Mina minnesbilder. 1. Nilsson, Birgit. 2. Women singers—
Biography. I. Title. ML420.N697A33   782.1′092′4 [B] ISBN: 0-385-14835-6 Library of
Congress Catalog Card Number 78–22343 Translation copyright © 1981 by Doubleday &
Company, Inc. First Edition in the United States of America All rights reserved

DESIGNED BY BEVERLEY VAWTER GALLEGOS

Contents

An attempt at a foreword

One rainy afternoon between two series of guest performances, I was sitting at a large table in my home in Skåne, in southern Sweden, trying to organize my newspaper clippings. They tend to accumulate in fairly substantial heaps, for it is only at irregular intervals that I get around to pasting them into big scrapbooks.

This is not the case, however, with my collection of pictures and photographs. These are stuffed, unsorted, into envelopes that then wind up in bureau drawers and old suitcases. And there they lie, although I do dip into them occasionally when I have to find some particular picture or when I am suddenly struck by a nostalgic wish to relive some episode in my varied past.

Gradually this sea of pictures has grown to such proportions that I find myself virtually inundated. Some of them I have acquired myself or been given by the concert societies and opera companies with which I've appeared, many have been given to me by friendly photographers and journalists, and quite a number have been sent to me by fans all over the world.

What occurred to me that rainy afternoon was that some of these pictures might interest my public, might even make up the backbone of an autobiography in pictures. And so I was forced to begin sorting them. I'm sorry to say that a lot of good photographs had to be consigned back to the bureau drawers indefinitely, and I'm sure there are some still lying there that I never even saw. I have often wondered how many pictures have been taken of me over the years.

The result, in any case, is this album of pictures, captions, and commentary. Finding a story line in the life of a peripatetic soprano is not of course the easiest thing in the world, but it seemed natural to begin with childhood and youth and the first years of my career. Soon, however, I was forced to abandon chronological order and concentrate instead on particular topics.

If this book succeeds in awakening pleasant memories in some of the people who have given me their applause and their admiration through the years, then it will have accomplished its purpose.

Birgit Nilsson

I grew up on a farm in Svenstad in the parish of West Karup on the Bjäre peninsula, not far from where my home province of Skåne meets the province of Halland on the west coast of Sweden. Until my grandfather turned the farm over to my father, we lived on a neighboring farm, where I was born. I was two years old when we moved to the farm in the picture, which has been in the family since the seventeenth century, or for at least as long as Skåne has been Swedish.

A cavalryman named Wahlberg, in the army of Charles XII, was quartered on the farm according to the custom of the time, and he married the daughter of the house. I am the seventh generation after Wahlberg. At one time the place belonged to a Woman with a capital W. Her name was Olu, a widow with an exceptionally strong and commanding personality. Ever since her day—in the 1700s—the farm has been known as Oles, and the addition of a Christian name produced Oles Sven (my grandfather's father), Oles Petter (my grandfather), Oles Nils (my father), and, until I began to be known in Sweden simply as Birgit, I was Oles Birgit. So even way back then a woman could make her voice heard in a man's world! The only thing it required was that she be much better than the men . . .

In the picture here to the left I am about three years old. I remember that I absolutely did not want to be photographed alone. How times change . . . The girl holding me is named Karin. She came to our farm as a vacation child from a poor home in Gothenburg and stayed until she married the well-to-do farmer who owned the place where I was born. As I was an only child, she came to be a sort of big sister to me.

My childhood home

Long days in the long rows of the beet fields. It was terribly dreary work. So I made up my mind: "Anything but farming!" That's me on the far left in the cap.

Twenty-one and still very unsure about what I was going to be.

Amateur theatre in the neighboring parish of Hov. I'm the one in the middle in the white dress. The boy with the basket on the left is my rejected suitor—in the play. I've forgotten what the play was called, but there was a cat in it called Petrus. A short time later I got a white cat of my own, and naturally I called him Petrus. He lived to be old and fat.

One day in the summer of 1941 there was a sudden terrible thunderstorm. Harvesting had to be interrupted while everyone tried to find shelter, including this charming family (left), Professor Bertil Lindqvist with his wife and two children, who happened to be passing by on bicycles. We gave them coffee and sweet rolls, and my father, as usual, suggested I entertain them with a song. I never needed much coaxing . . . They were very enthusiastic and offered to take care of me when I went up to Stockholm in the fall for an audition at the Academy of Music. They were infinitely kind and helpful and let me stay with them until I could find a place of my own.

Lilian Lindqvist, B.N., Bertil Lindqvist, my mother, and the Lindqvist children, Ulf and Ulla.

In the quiet bosom of my family. I'm working on a piece of very fine needle-point for my dowry. I still haven't finished it . . .

My first car—a Fiat 500, dark blue with red side-walls. I've owned many cars since, of various makes and colors, but never one I was more attached to. I called him Putte.

My first concert dress

was made in Stockholm for a jubilee concert at the old Bourse. Among those present was Crown Prince Gustaf Adolf, as he was then. The next day in *Stockholms-Tidningen*, Gunnar Mascoll Silfverstolpe, a member of the Swedish Academy, wrote a poem about my performance that ran something like this:

Birgit Nilsson and accompanist were the next to
    follow,
Radiant in white, a worthy priestess of Apollo,
She sang for us (and suddenly we understood
    the Sirens' power to enamor)
Songs by Sjögren, Alfvén, Petterson-Berger, and
    Stenhammar.

Afterward there was a ball in the Hall of Mirrors at the Grand Hotel, and I wore this white gown and jewelry lent me by my landlady on Riddargatan. I danced with, among others, Isaac Grünewald, one of Sweden's most famous painters. He told me I had a diamond in my throat but that it needed polishing to remove the carbon it still bore.

My fee for that performance was fifty crowns. The dress cost three times that. I wore it again on many different occasions and eventually dyed it black to give it a new lease on life. Sharp-eyed readers will recognize the dyed version a little farther on in this book.

The little apartment on Birger Jarlsgatan that I shared with a girl from home, an artist named Signe Lundquist, later Signe Lanje. She was one of the most diligent people I've ever met. There was nothing she wasn't willing to deny herself in order to paint. In fact, her unbelievable energy always gave me a guilty conscience. But I too had to deny myself a great deal, though I must say I was only too glad to give up thinning beets . . . there are limits!

Lower left: Snapshot from the Opera School show in 1946. The two gentlemen in the middle of the back row, one on either side of Eva Prytz, are, on the left, Kurt Bendix, Royal Opera conductor in Stockholm, and, on the right, Ragnar Hyltén-Cavallius, who became Director of Production. Both were teachers at the school. I myself am in the middle row at the far right. Some readers may recognize others in the group as well, for all of them pursued operatic careers at least for a time. Just to the right of Hyltén-Cavallius, for example, is Eva Gustafsson, who sang Amneris in Toscanini's recording of *Aïda*.

Below: The trio from *Der Rosenkavalier* at the Opera School show in 1946. Left to right: Eva Prytz as Sophie, Ingrid Eksell as Octavian, and myself as the Marschallin.

Nose dive

My opera debut—as Agathe in Weber's *Der Freischütz*, on October 9, 1946—was a substitution on three days' notice, and I paid for it dearly in nerves and tears. Harald André was General Manager at the time, and the director was Anders Henrikson. I was poorly prepared, of course, and could not possibly do my very best under the circumstances. Moreover I had a conductor—Leo Blech—who was seventy-five years old and had long since forgotten what it was like to be young and inexperienced. I've had a certain aversion for conductors of the "Prussian" school ever since. In ten minutes, a conductor like that can rob me of all my self-confidence.

Fortunately none of this was apparent to the critics, who gave me fine reviews the next day. But the Royal Opera put me on ice, labeled "unmusical and untalented."

With three exceptions—Electra in *Idomeneo*, Leonore in *Fidelio*, and Amelia in *Un Ballo in Maschera*—I have sung all my roles for the first time at the Royal Opera in Stockholm, most of them in Swedish.

KUNGL. TEATERN

Onsdagen den 9 oktober 1946 kl. 20

Gästdirigent: Hovkapellmästare LEO BLECH

Gästregissör: ANDERS HENRIKSON

För 400:de gången:

FRISKYTTEN

Romantisk opera i 3 akter (2:a och 3:e akterna avdelade i 2 tablåer) av F. Kind.
Musiken av C. M. von Weber.
Dekorationer och kostymer efter skisser av Bo Beskow.
Sceentekniska anordningar av Gunnar Broberg.

Ottokar, böhmisk furste	Georg Svedenbrant
Kuno, furstlig jägmästare	Sven-Erik Jacobsson
Agathe, hans dotter	Birgit Nilsson (debut)
Anna, hennes släkting	Eva Prytz
Kaspar } jägare, anställda hos Kuno	Sigurd Björling
Max }	Conny Söderström
En eremit	Folke Jonsson
Kilian, en rik bonde	Simon Edwardsen
Den Svarte Jägaren	Folke Rydberg
Brudtärnan	Florence Widgren

Jägare och furstens svit. Lantfolk och musikanter.
Brudtärnor.

Kl. **20**—omkr. 22.40

Wearing "the hat." It was the prettiest hat I ever owned. The year was 1948. Harald André, who was General Manager of the Stockholm Opera, ordered me to interrupt my vacation and audition for Edward Johnson, then General Manager of the Metropolitan. So I took the train up to Stockholm—on the Sunday my banns were read in church for the second time—and strode boldly out on stage in the hat. This very nearly proved disastrous, for right in the middle of a high C at the climax of an aria from *Un Ballo in Maschera*, the hat almost fell off. I caught it at the last moment, but there was no suppressing the general merriment. Mr. Johnson complimented me, first for my hat, then for my voice, and said he felt that I should continue to study the Italian repertoire.

Many people through the years have claimed to be my "discoverer," but the only one who really earned the title was Ragnar Blennow, a voice teacher and choir director from the town of Åstorp. The first time I sang for him, he turned to me and burst out, "Miss Nilsson, believe me, you are unquestionably going to be a great singer!" And he didn't stop there. He took me by the collar and saw to it that I had an audition at the Royal College of Music in Stockholm. He was an exceptional teacher and helped greatly to prepare me for my coming studies. He was also an impressive personality, with a hasty temper. I had great respect for him and I also loved him dearly.

Left: Beethoven's Ninth at the Concert Society in Stockholm, 1948. Left to right: Sigurd Björling, B.N., conductor Erich Kleiber, Lisa Tunell, Gösta Bäckelin, and Concert Hall Director Johannes Norrby.

Wedding . . .

Just the two of us, at the Swedish Church in Copenhagen on September 10, 1948. We met on a train from Skåne to Stockholm in 1945. Bertil Niklasson was studying veterinary medicine, and I was studying voice and was on my way to Stockholm to make my debut at the Concert Hall, with Tor Mann conducting. Three years later we were married.

. . . and silver wedding

Twenty-five years later we celebrated our silver anniversary in Bangkok. The Thais have a custom of setting a caged bird free on important occasions of this kind. Our friends supplied us with a cage and a bird, and we dutifully gave it its liberty. I have no idea what this ceremony is supposed to signify, but I think I can safely say that in twenty-five years of marriage neither one of us ever felt like a bird in a cage.

My first Verdi role, Lady Macbeth, 1947 . . .

Donna Anna in *Don Giovanni*   Lisa in *Queen of Spades*

The years at the Stockholm Opera

My real breakthrough came as Lady Macbeth in 1947. Another young singer named Inga Sundström was originally assigned the role but fell ill, and five weeks before the premiere the Opera was left without a leading lady. Fritz Busch was conducting, and his son Hans was the director. Hans Busch had heard of me and asked me to audition for him. He was full of enthusiasm, but we had a hard time convincing Harald André, who was then General Manager. As it turned out, the Busches and I worked together splendidly, and my career was begun. I sang ten performances in three weeks. It is a marvelous role, this Lady Macbeth, and I looked forward to every performance the way a child looks forward to Christmas.

After my success as Lady Macbeth, new parts came thick and fast. Even Leo Blech, who was directing *Tannhäuser*, decided to take a chance and offered me the part of Venus. I played opposite the world-famous Wagnerian tenor Set Svanholm, and once again I was well received by the public and the critics.

From the fall of 1948, I was a Resident Artist with the Royal Swedish Opera Company. In the spring of 1949 I sang Donna Anna in *Don Giovanni*. Shortly before the premiere, my mother was killed in an automobile accident. I had to interrupt the rehearsals for a time, but they were counting on me to sing on opening night, and I did.

I have sung Donna Anna in three languages—Swedish, German, and Italian. It was the first role I ever sang in Italy—in Florence, over the New Year, 1951–52.

Also in 1949 I sang Lisa in Tchaikovsky's *Queen of Spades*. Issay Dobrowen directed and conducted. He was an incredibly forceful and inspiring man. I was new at the game, and I could feel his fiery Russian temperament at the podium was prompting me to strain my voice, but working with him was extremely interesting and stimulating. Isa Quensel played the Countess, and Einar Beyron, father of the famous Swedish singer Catarina Ligendza, sang the unhappy Herman, who forsakes Lisa for the gaming tables.

Right: A rehearsal picture from *Queen of Spades*—Isa Quensel, Einar Beyron, Issay Dobrowen, and B.N.

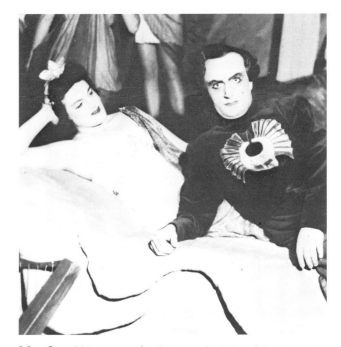

My first Wagner role, Venus, in *Tannhäuser*, 1947.

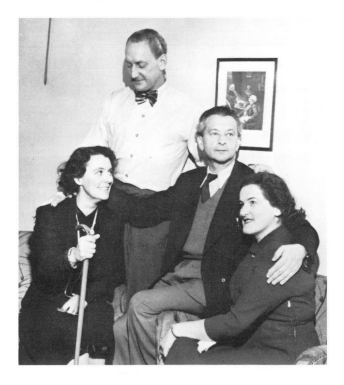

Glyndebourne 1951

Fritz Busch, who was Musical Director of the Glyndebourne Festival Opera, had not forgotten me, and in 1951 he engaged me for the part of Electra in Mozart's *Idomeneo*. I arrived in Glyndebourne on my birthday, May 17. The heating in postwar England was not all it might have been, and I found myself shivering with cold. The only spot with a trace of warmth was the greenhouse, and there I spent the greater part of my birthday.

Glyndebourne is a charming place in Sussex, some miles south of London. The manor house is surrounded by a well-tended park and luxuriant meadows, and cows graze peacefully right up to the very doors. I loved the quiet pace of the work and the tranquillity of the setting. But it was hard to tell if you were really at work or taking a vacation.

Idomeneo is a lovely opera with glorious choral parts and wonderful solo passages. The title role was sung by the fine English tenor Richard Lewis, Leopold Simoneau was a first-rate Idamante, and the part of Ilia was beautifully sung by young Sena Jurinac. My own role was very dramatic, and the grand aria toward the end was particularly demanding. The picture below, left, shows me, Leopold Simoneau, and Sena Jurinac on the steps of the manor house.

At the same time that I was performing at Glyndebourne, Set Svanholm was appearing as Tristan at Covent Garden in London, with Kirsten Flagstad singing Isolde. I somehow managed to get my hands on a ticket to the premiere and Fritz Busch let me out of rehearsals at Glyndebourne. I will never forget what an enormous impression the performance made on me. I was deeply impressed by Flagstad's voice, which had the power of an organ. Little did I dream that two years later I myself would get the chance to sing Isolde, much less that I would get a very complimentary letter from Kirsten Flagstad, who heard me sing the role on the radio shortly after my debut.

In the picture below, Set is brightening our lives at Glyndebourne. On the right is Isa Quensel, a Swedish soprano and actress who sang Despina in *Così fan tutte* at Glyndebourne that season.

Elisabeth

Isolde

Salome

Salome, 1954. One of my best parts. But in the beginning I was dead set against singing it. All the odds seemed to be against me. I had just recovered from a bad case of pleurisy and had some adhesions in my right lung. My breathing was distinctly impaired, and I doubted I would be able to perform the long and difficult Dance of the Seven Veils. But the director, Göran Gentele, turned on all his charm and talked me into it. We worked like slaves. He rehearsed me in every step, every gesture, and in the end I managed to identify with the cruelly perverse Princess Salome. Sixten Ehrling conducted magnificently, and the opera was a huge success. Shortly afterwards, I was named Royal Court Singer by King Gustaf VI Adolf, who attended the performance several times. Once Queen Louise—the former Louise Mountbatten—came with him. She may have been a trifle shocked, because she covered her eyes when Jokanaan's head was lifted out of the well on a silver tray. There actually began to develop a sort of Birgit Nilsson fever in Stockholm. There was even a carpet company that named a rug Salome. Those were glorious days.

I sang my first Elisabeth in *Tannhäuser* and my first Isolde in 1953. All dramatic sopranos dream of singing Isolde, and I was overjoyed when the Opera allowed me to take on the role when the superb Brita Hertzberg—the mother of Catarina Ligendza—left it. The director was Rudolf Hartmann, General Manager of the Bavarian State Opera in Munich, and the conductor was Herbert Sandberg, Leo Blech's son-in-law and an exceptional musical coach. My Isolde has no doubt added new hues to her palette over the years, but many people have said that even in 1953 my performance was amazingly mature and fully realized.

My first Brünnhilde in Die Walküre . . .

Since 1949 I had always sung Sieglinde in *Die Walküre*, and it was with a heavy heart that I had to give up that role in 1955 in order to succeed Brita Hertzberg and climb into the armor and the helmet of the Val-kyrie. I had sung the other two Brünn-hildes—in *Siegfried* and in *Götterdäm-merung*—since 1949 and 1954, respec-tively. By now I suppose I must have sung about a hundred and sixty *Walküres*, with many different Wotans. But never with one who had greater warmth and sincerity than Sigurd Björling.

I sang my first Leonore in *Fidelio* in the summer of 1953. It was my second major appearance abroad—at the festival at Bad Hersfeld in West Germany. My Florestan was the Danish-born tenor Helge Ros-waenge (lower picture), who had a special following in Germany and Austria.

The conductor at Bad Hersfeld was Robert Heger of the Bavarian State Opera. I didn't dare tell him until the opening was over and all had gone well that I had never sung *Fidelio* before. The festival took place in the ruins of an old church that Napo-leon's cavalry once made camp in and acci-dentally set on fire. The remaining walls made the most fantastic backdrop for *Fi-delio*. The evenings were mild and the moon shed its magic light on a sparsely lighted stage, producing a mood and atmos-phere that I've never experienced in any other production. Every time I hear the third *Leonore* overture, those wonderful evenings in Bad Hersfeld come back to me all over again.

. . . and my first Fidelio

Bayreuth

The first time I ever approached this "sacred" building, I did so with enormous awe and respect. As I climbed the long, steep hill to the Festspielhaus, it was not merely the exertion that made my heart pound. I was almost overcome by nervousness and excitement. How would I ever manage to sing in this Wagnerian temple? I almost imagined that those who sang there were not ordinary mortals but a tribe of gods and goddesses. My expectations were so exaggerated that I was nearly disappointed by the first performances I saw. The artists were human beings with failings and faults, just like me and everyone else. Gradually my nerves calmed, but the awe and respect stayed with me all the sixteen summers I sang in Bayreuth.

Incidentally, I did not make my Bayreuth debut in an operatic role but rather in the soprano part in Beethoven's *Ninth Symphony*, under the direction of Paul Hindemith, in 1953.

A scene from the second act of *Lohengrin* with Wolfgang Windgassen as Lohengrin and, in the background, Ludwig Weber as the King. Elsa was my first operatic role at Bayreuth, in 1954.

The new Bayreuth style was very statuesque. The idea was to pare away all gesture and let the character work from the inside out, so to speak. Here, under Wolfgang's supervision, I am learning to make my first-act entrance as Elsa. The man standing in the background is Hermann Weigert, married to Astrid Varnay. He was the most phenomenal *répétiteur* and coach I ever worked with. Sadly, he died the following year.

Opposite: Three role portraits from Bayreuth. Left to right: Isolde in Wolfgang's *Tristan*, 1957; in Wieland's, 1962; and, Brünnhilde in Wieland's production of *Die Walküre*, 1965.

The Swedish soprano Nanny Larsén-Todsen—a brilliant Brünnhilde and Isolde—was called the uncrowned queen of Bayreuth in the 1920s and early 1930s. We are here exchanging a few words outside the Festspielhaus. She is now ninety-six years old and lives in Stockholm.

The Bayreuth Festival did not reopen after the war until 1951, under the direction of the brothers Wieland and Wolfgang Wagner, the grandsons of the master. The latter handled administration and finances, while Wieland (1917–66), whose inclinations were exclusively artistic, staged the productions—an enormous task when one considers that he did it virtually alone and that he also designed the sets. However, it wasn't long before Wolfgang (born 1919) wanted to try his luck as a director and set designer, and in 1954 I sang Elsa in his production of *Lohengrin.*

It was not always easy to understand what Wolfgang wanted. In addition, he spoke very fast and in a dialect—Oberfränkisch—that even native Germans found difficult to grasp. With my poor German, I understood no more than half or even a third of what he said. But somehow we managed.

The Wagner brothers were not excessively compatible. If you were a success in Wolfgang's productions, Wieland's attitude became cold, almost hostile. In 1957, Wolfgang was going to stage a new production of *Tristan und Isolde* and offered me the role of Isolde. I curtsied and accepted gratefully.

The conductor was the talented young Wolfgang Sawallisch. He rehearsed us intensely, polished us hard, and got the results we all wanted. A *succès pyramidal.* The only sour note was that some critics were unhappy with Wolfgang's sets. The first act, for example, with its transparent plastic walls, was likened to a photographer's studio. Wolfgang Windgassen sang Tristan beau-

tifully, and, as Brangäne, Grace Hoffman was utterly captivating.

It was not until 1962 that I got to work with Wieland, the older brother, in a new production of *Tristan.* As a result of my success as Isolde under Wolfgang, Wieland avoided offering me the part in his own production and tried instead to find someone new. I knew perfectly well what was going through his mind, but that didn't prevent my feeling saddened and hurt. After searching the whole world for a new Isolde for months, in vain, he finally offered the part to me. For once I swallowed my pride and accepted.

So at last we stood face to face, like two fighting cocks—he the genius, and I the world-famous star. Which of us would bend? His reaction was somewhat sour when I declared that I was prepared to forget all of my previous eighty-seven Isoldes in order to create a new one with him. It was only after an hour's work or more that the unyielding expression on his face began to brighten. We had found one another.

It was a wonderful week we spent together giving birth to an original and yet, for me, perfectly natural Isolde. He shaped the role to my temperament, that is to say, to my particular capacities. He somehow tailor-made the part for me. The usual practice elsewhere is for directors and even costumers to work out their designs long before they have any idea what artists they will be working with. If a role or a costume turns out to fit too tightly, then it is the offending body that has to be altered . . . A director simply does not compromise his principles, for that could all too easily be seen as a concession, or even as a defeat.

Under Wieland's direction, Isolde had very nearly the fury of an Elektra in Act I, while at the same time her love for Tristan could always be heard in her voice and seen in her every gesture. Wolfgang Windgassen, with his controlled Bayreuth acting style, was once again an ideal Tristan, and Kerstin Meyer was a submissive and self-sacrificing Brangäne. Wieland often said later in interviews and conversation that this *Tristan und Isolde* was as close as he would ever come to his ideal. Last but not least, Karl Böhm conducted. I have had some of my greatest triumphs with Böhm on the podium, and this was one. His interpretation of *Tristan* was a declaration of love from beginning to end.

At a rehearsal with Kerstin Meyer and Wieland Wagner.

Wieland demonstrates his conception of Isolde's "Spottlied" in the first act.

Rehearsing with Wieland
Wagner: Brünnhilde's
awakening in *Siegfried*.

Some photographs of Wieland Wagner's 1962 Bayreuth production of *Tristan und Isolde*. He was his own set designer. Above: Isolde gives Tristan the drink in the first act, as Brangäne watches.

Left: The love duet in Act II. My Tristan here is Wolfgang Windgassen, an incomparable Wagnerian tenor.

Right: Isolde's "Liebestod." I gave my last performance at Bayreuth in this production, in August 1970, after sixteen seasons of hard work and unforgettable experiences. It was the final performance of Wieland's *Tristan*, and I didn't want to sing in any other.

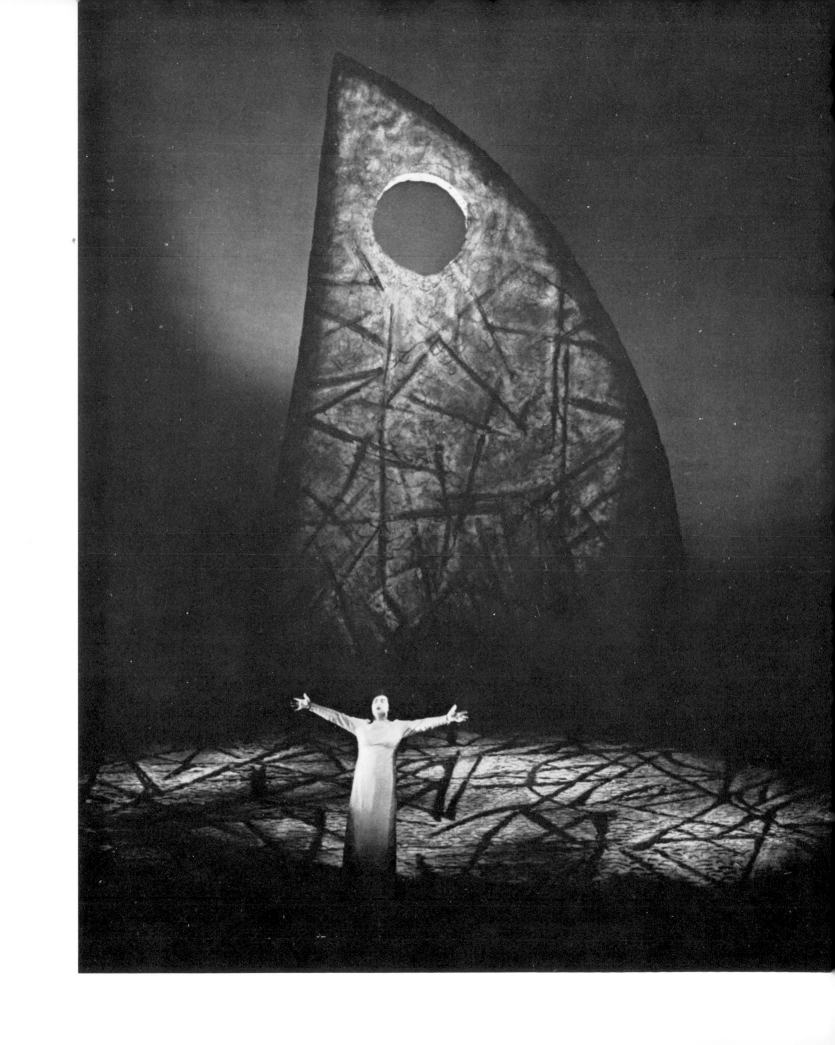

In 1965 came a new production of *The Ring of the Nibelungen*, this time under the direction of Wieland Wagner. Once again the rehearsals were enormously interesting, in spite of the fact that Wieland was already showing the signs of serious illness. He had hoped to do further work on the production the following year—although it was tremendously effective from the beginning—but by then he was in the hospital. His death in 1966 was a hard blow to the world of opera. He worked not only in Bayreuth but also in Stuttgart, Berlin, Hamburg, Vienna, and Paris, among other cities, and he produced not only his grandfather's works but those of other composers as well.

Theo Adam (right) was a young and animated Wotan. It was not easy to succeed Hans Hotter, who had become a legend at Bayreuth, but with Wieland, Adam created an entirely new Wotan, not at all like Hotter's somewhat theatrical interpretation.

Leaving the stage door at Bayreuth with my famous makeup case, whose story I tell on the last page of this book.

Above right: Karl Böhm once threatened not to come back to Bayreuth the following year, but Windgassen and I managed to change his mind. After the final curtain of the summer, we fell on our knees and begged Maestro Böhm to conduct *Tristan* again the next season, and our plea was successful. In the background, center, is the incredibly gifted choral director Wilhelm Pitz, a master of his art, honored as few others in Bayreuth for his accomplishments. Both Windgassen and Pitz died several years ago, at the height of their artistic careers.

Performances were often followed by lovely parties, formal and informal. In the picture at the right I am chatting with Frau Dr. Hilger (center), wife of the president of the Richard Wagner Verband, and Winifred Wagner, the widow of Siegfried Wagner, who was the son of Richard and Cosima. Winifred was the mother of Wieland and Wolfgang and a woman of uncommon charm and vitality, very outspoken, whom the press surrounded with a hint of scandal, partly because of her friendship with Adolf Hitler. No inconsequential figure in Bayreuth, she lived in Siegfried Wagner Haus, a wing of Haus Wahnfried. She died in March 1980 at the age of eighty-two.

Right: A pleasant interlude with the Begum Aga Khan, an elegant and impressive woman with a great interest in music. She has missed very few season openings since the Festival resumed in 1951.

More draft horse than diva

My debut at the Teatro alla Scala in Milan took place in the spring of 1958, when I sang Brünnhilde in *Die Walküre*. But the biggest event of my life, up to then, occurred on the seventh of December that same year when I opened the season as Turandot. I was the first non-Italian ever granted such an honor, and of course I was terribly proud and happy. On the day of the opening, Milan was covered with such dense fog that it seemed difficult to breathe. The fog found its way into the theatre itself, which was decked with thousands of carnations, and considerably dulled the glitter of the women's magnificent jewelry. Formal attire was still compulsory for gentlemen, and everyone of wealth, name, or title was on hand.

As I toiled up the long staircase with my incredibly heavy, forty-foot (!) train, I felt more like a draft horse than a diva. I was, to put it mildly, uncomfortable. I was having trouble breathing, and I thought I must sound dreadful. Moreover, I was well upstage, whereas Calaf—sung by the famous tenor Giuseppe di Stefano (right)—was down by the footlights. So I was prepared for the same feeble applause that followed the first act, in which Turandot merely appears and does not sing. But I don't suppose I have ever been more surprised in all my life. The last note of the second act had hardly died away before the audience leaped to their feet, shouted, cheered, and embraced one another. In other words, this very aristocratic audience behaved like perfect lunatics. My career was made, and one more star had apparently been born on Italy's preeminent operatic stage.

A gala evening at La Scala —opening night of the 370th season, 1958. This was the evening that I made a name for myself as Turandot.

31

Salome was another of my great successes at La Scala. I sang it there in 1967. The production was an old one, originally from Munich, where it had its premiere in 1955 with me in the title role. I did not do the dance on that occasion, but I did do it in Milan. Professor Rudolf Hartmann, General Manager of the Bavarian State Opera, directed in both cases, and it gave me a feeling of security to have Berislav Klobučar conducting at La Scala.

Opposite: Doctor Antonio Ghiringhelli, then General Manager of La Scala, gives me a hug onstage after a performance of *Salome*. He would often linger in my dressing room after a performance and tell me stories about himself, including stories of his amorous adventures. I could never figure out just how interested he was in opera. His office was often empty during the day, and negotiations with singers were always handled by Signor Luigi Oldani, one of his assistants. Only rarely did Ghiringhelli visit a rehearsal or a performance. He was very wealthy, however, and when La Scala needed to be restored after the damage it suffered in the war, he is said to have made no paltry contribution.

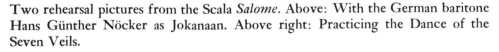

Two rehearsal pictures from the Scala *Salome*. Above: With the German baritone Hans Günther Nöcker as Jokanaan. Above right: Practicing the Dance of the Seven Veils.

Right: An audience at the Vatican with His Holiness Pope Pius XII, a great Wagner enthusiast, in 1958. I was in Rome for·a guest appearance in *Die Walküre*. Third from the left is Sigurd Björling, who was singing Wotan, then B.N. Between me and the Pope, peering over his right shoulder, is Leonie Rysanek, who sang Sieglinde. Fifth from the right is Ira Malaniuk (Fricka), and third from the right, Ludwig Weber, who sang a marvelous Hunding.

In the presidential box after the opening night of *Turandot* in 1958. Left to right: Conductor Antonio Votto, General Manager Ghiringhelli, B.N., Prince Bernhard of the Netherlands, Italy's President Giovanni Gronchi, and Rosanna Carteri, who sang Liù.

Vienna—city of my dreams

Yes, the fact is that Vienna has become just about my favorite city in the world. In the spring when clusters of lilacs hang heavy and fragrant in all the parks, and ducks are out taking their ducklings for their first swim, and familiar melodies float through the dusk from small Viennese orchestras, or in the fall when sunshine and warmth linger on much longer than they do in Scandinavia and I have wandered out to Grinzing, perhaps, to enjoy a *Heurigen*, and this first wine of the year, still fermenting, sparkles in my glass like champagne—as such times Vienna has a special attraction for me. Despite its 1,600,000 inhabitants, the city seems intimate and relaxing. The Viennese, with their charm and joie de vivre, refuse to be trapped in the treadmill of big-city life. They dare to be alive and human.

The Viennese have a great cultural heritage and a multitude of traditions to watch over and take pride in, but I do not think I exaggerate when I say that the apple of their eye is the Vienna State Opera. Built in 1869, it was almost totally destroyed in March 1945, in the final weeks of the war. But it was completely restored, and, on November 5, 1955, rededicated. A month earlier, the Burgtheater, too, was reopened after an almost equally extensive restoration. Poor, war-torn Austria had somehow found the means to rebuild two large theatres!

I entered Vienna for the first time in the spring of 1954. What met my eye was not the gay Vienna of Emperor Franz Josef and the Habsburgs that one has heard so much about but an impoverished and mutilated city. The Russians and the other three great powers still occupied all the large buildings and hotels. Visitors had to find accommodations either privately or in small, drafty hotels and pensions. On my first visit, I usually slept with my fur coat on . . .

For ten years after the war, opera was performed at the Theater an der Wien. It was at this rather small theatre, built in 1801, that Mozart's *Magic Flute* became a box-office bonanza for librettist and theatre manager Emanuel Schikaneder ten years after Mozart's death. It is also the theatre where Beethoven's *Fidelio* was first performed—in the midst of Napoleon's siege of Vienna—and where many Strauss and Lehár operettas had their premieres.

On this stage I was to give guest performances in four different roles in nine days, singing all of them in their original languages for the first time! I was to sing Elsa in *Lohengrin*, Elisabeth in *Tannhäuser*, Sieglinde in *Die Walküre*—all in German—and Aïda in Italian. Rehearsals were practically nonexistent, and as a rule I didn't meet the artists I was singing opposite until the evening of the performance. The director I ran into more or less in passing. He told me where to make my entrances and exits and concluded magnificently, "Otherwise, just remember that we perform in the spirit of Wagner!" Bewildered, I thanked him for this somewhat laconic advice and began to get ready for that evening's performance. Lohengrin was being sung by the famous Max Lorenz, who, several evenings later, also sang Siegmund in *Die Walküre*. He looked like a god but was also a very sweet and amiable man. In fact, he was the only one of the soloists who deigned to speak to me. He even knew a few words of Swedish, souvenirs of a guest appearance in the *Ring* in Stockholm in 1936. They weren't exactly the sort of words he had learned from someone's maiden aunt, but in my loneliness they were like music to my ears. Tannhäuser was sung by Wolfgang Windgassen, and *Aïda* was conducted by a likable young conductor who impressed me greatly even then—Berislav Klobučar.

Apparently my performances made a good impression, because only a month later I was back to sing Senta in *The Flying Dutchman* and my second Sieglinde. This time I was accompanied from Stockholm by Sigurd Björling, who sang both the Dutchman and Wotan. Five minutes before the curtain went up on *The Flying Dutchman*, the conductor, Rudolf Kempe, came rushing into my dressing room to ask if I had been told about the cuts in the music. Naturally no one had said a word. That whole evening my brain was occupied primarily with keeping track of all the jumps. It was ghastly!

Just before Christmas that same year I was back again, to sing Isolde. Karl Böhm, who had been made General Manager that fall, saw the performance. According to the present General Manager, Professor Egon Seefehlner, who was then his chief assistant, Böhm is supposed to have said, "But she is a *soubrette!*" Nevertheless, he called me to his office the next day, praised me lavishly, and engaged me to sing Donna Anna in *Don Giovanni* in Naples in the spring of 1955.

My first premiere in Vienna came in the spring of 1957—now in the "new" opera house—as Brünnhilde in *Die Walküre*. Up to then I had sung repertory productions, with very few rehearsals or none at all. Now for the first time I got to work on a production "from the bottom up," and I was delighted. Herbert von Karajan, who had succeeded Böhm as General Manager, conducted and directed. There were a great many lighting rehearsals but considerably fewer musical ones. The cast was splendid, with Hans Hotter himself as Wotan. He looked like a Greek god and gave a very impressive performance. Karajan was then, perhaps, at the height of his musical career. His *Walküre* was vibrant with life and passion, and not a single bar lacked its own inner excitement. The performance was musically so thrilling that it more than made up for all the tedious technical rehearsals.

Strolling in Vienna with the evening's Tristan, Jon Vickers.

The Viennese have a very particular taste in music. No *forte* or *fortissimo* will throw them into such raptures as a well-sung *pianissimo*. The first time I performed Aïda in Vienna, in 1954, I sang the high C in the Nile aria *forte*. The applause that followed was mostly dutiful. At the next performance I decided to sing it *pianissimo*, and I thought the applause would never end. Had I sung the same note *pianissimo* at La Scala, I'm sure not a hand would have moved . . .

Left: Aïda in Vienna, 1954. Right: Brünnhilde in *Die Walküre*, Vienna, 1957.

A dramatic moment in *Fidelio* in Vienna. Leonore, disguised as a man and using the name Fidelio, rushes out with a pistol and, at the last moment, prevents her captive husband, Florestan, from being murdered by the villain, Pizarro. Here Florestan is the American tenor James McCracken. He began his career as a tenor in the chorus at the Metropolitan, and it was several years before he dared take the big step and stand on his own two feet. He studied in Italy, made a name for himself in Europe, and returned to the Met as a star.

After *Die Walküre*, in 1957, there were productions of *Siegfried* and *Götterdämmerung* in the years that followed, all three directed and conducted by Karajan. The last of these operas is the most difficult—musically as well as theatrically. And so all of us—the technical staff in particular, perhaps—heaved a sigh of relief when, after seventy-eight lighting rehearsals and two orchestra rehearsals, the premiere finally took place.

The year 1968 proved to be full of honors and distinctions. In Vienna I was made simultaneously Austrian *Kammersängerin* and Honorary Member of the Vienna State Opera, an uncommon distinction, especially for a foreigner. The other twenty-odd honorary members were predominantly Austrian, and my delight and pride knew no bounds. Below, in the presence of other honorary members and notables, the Minister of Education, Theodor Piffl-Perčevič, presents me with the two certificates.

Brünnhilde in *Götterdämmerung*.

What a ring!

In 1968, the standing-room audience in Vienna and I became "engaged." For the premiere of *Tristan und Isolde* they took up a collection and had this gold ring made, with its engraving of Isolde's head. Over the years I have been given innumerable tokens of esteem, but few have moved and pleased me as much as this one. After the performance, at least three hundred people escorted me to the Hotel Europa, where I was staying. They filled the entire street and square and stopped the traffic. It seemed hard to leave these fans at the hotel with a simple thank-you and good-night, so I stood at the top of the steps and made a little impromptu speech, in which I returned their declaration of love by promising always to be faithful to my Viennese public. When a person has had the privilege and the joy of being the declared favorite of the Viennese for as many years as I, such a promise is easy to keep.

The Vienna State Opera was opened in 1869, an event that had to be celebrated a hundred years later. Here I am at the festivities with Austria's Chancellor, Dr. Josef Klaus.

At a dinner given by the Finnish Ambassador in Vienna, Jussi Mäkkinen. Among the guests, U.N. Secretary-General Kurt Waldheim, Mrs. Waldheim, and B.N. During the time Herr Waldheim was Austrian Ambassador to the United Nations in New York, I was also invited to sample their generous hospitality.

The Swedish ambassadors in Vienna have always taken good care of me. Baron Karl-Gustaf Lagerfelt, a great opera lover, was particularly considerate, and we became good friends. He was a generous host and often gave lovely dinners and small suppers in his home. This picture, above right, is from a party he gave for a number of opera enthusiasts and artists after a performance of *Turandot*. In the middle, our host himself. On the right, the delightful Hilde Güden, one of the darlings of the Viennese public. On the far left at the back, over my right shoulder, you can just catch a glimpse of another guest, Mr. Bruno Kreisky, the Chancellor of Austria.

Over the years I have sung in three different productions of *Tristan und Isolde* in Vienna. The third, which had its premiere just before Christmas in 1968, was, in my opinion, the most beautiful. Karl Böhm conducted, and August Everding directed. Everding, now General Manager of the Bavarian State Opera in Munich after several years as head of the opera in Hamburg, has told me since how terribly nervous and frightened he was. By 1968 I had sung Isolde perhaps a hundred and fifty times, while he was directing his first opera. But the result was dazzling. Everding is an extremely stimulating director, and singers love to work with him.

The way to see Vienna in style is to hire a couple of *Fiaker*—horse-drawn coaches—and take your friends on a sightseeing tour. At the height of spring, you might go all the way to Schönbrunn, the Prater, or the English Garden. It's not cheap, but when the tour is over the coachman will often take his leave with a chivalrous kiss of your hand and a friendly personal compliment or two. You'd be less than a woman if you didn't feel then that you'd had your money's worth.

At a *Heurigen*, in Grinzing, the idea is to eat, drink, and enjoy yourself, sing along or let yourself be entertained by the local talent. The two people enjoying themselves beside me in this picture are Bruno Kreisky, the Chancellor of Austria, and his wife, Vera. They lived in Sweden for several years during the Hitler era, and both of them speak Swedish. None of the other guests in the restaurant seemed to think there was anything remarkable about seeing the head of government in these *gemütlich* surroundings. The Kreiskys have an attractive but not especially luxurious house in Heiligenstadt, not far from Grinzing, and every now and then they spend an evening at a *Heurigen*—with friends or just by themselves. I couldn't help thinking about all the police and bodyguards and security checks there would be if the Chancellor of Germany were to visit such a place, not to mention the President of the United States.

Lovely Ulla Jacobsson, who starred in *One Summer of Happiness* and *Smiles of a Summer Night* in the 1950s, has lived in Vienna with her husband for many years.

During the long rehearsals of *The Ring of the Nibelungen*, my colleagues in London taught me to play skat, Richard Strauss's favorite card game. Left to right: Thomas Stewart, Wolfgang Windgassen, B.N., Gottlob Frick, and Hans Hotter. Occasionally I had beginner's luck and had just won a game when the photographer took this picture.

Conductors and managers in London

Every country, indeed every city, has its own customs and its own way of life. In the beginning I had a terrible time getting used to the incredible self-control of the English. I couldn't help smiling a bit at what struck me as their enormous self-esteem. Everything was better in England! After a series of futile temperamental outbursts, however, I discovered that that sort of behavior gets you nowhere. An Englishman only feels pity for people who cannot control their emotions. Once you realize this, you actually become much friendlier and nicer. And then even London can seem relaxing to a peripatetic soprano.

The Royal Opera House at Covent Garden is not one of the prettiest I've seen, at least not its exterior and the neighborhood it stands in. Until quite recently, it was surrounded by vegetable stalls and warehouses. If you weren't careful, you might slip on a bunch of old beet greens and fall right on your duff in front of the main entrance. Now, however, the stalls closest to Covent Garden have been banished to some other location. The opera house itself is old and worn, and the so-called prima donna's dressing room does not appear to have been repainted since about the year one. In the winter, the building is cold and drafty, and you have to bundle up well in wool sweaters between entrances.

When Beverly Sills was making her first guest appearance at Covent Garden and the General Administrator asked her if there was anything he could do to make her more comfortable, she said, "Yes, thanks, you could warm up the toilet seat for me!" She hasn't been back.

But at the present time Covent Garden has one of the best opera companies in the world. They have proper rehearsals, and they take the time to prepare performances thoroughly. Moreover, the theatre has ideal acoustics for a singer. Covent Garden has a wonderful "team," from the head of the opera to the stage-door porter. Sir John Tooley, the present General Administrator, is a very likable man and has won everyone's esteem and trust. His predecessor, Sir David Webster, was a splendid, jovial gentle-

Above: A dear colleague in the audience, Placido Domingo, visits me backstage in 1977.

A sweet gesture of appreciation from Sir John Tooley after the premiere of *Elektra* in May 1977.

man. He was head of the opera for twenty-five years and held the record at that time for longest reigning operatic general manager.

Sir Georg Solti, who was Musical Director of Covent Garden for ten years or so, did a great deal to raise the artistic standards. He conducted any number of superb premiere performances to enormous public acclaim. The English critics, however, never managed to discover his prodigious talent until he was about to leave, at which point they changed their tune and praised him to the skies. Musically, some of the most distinguished performances of *Elektra* in which I have ever taken part were at Covent Garden with Solti conducting. They stand out as high points in my career. Public and performers alike left the theatre breathless.

In 1977 I did *Elektra* at Covent Garden again. This time the conductor was Carlos Kleiber, the son of Erich Kleiber, for whom I sang in the late forties and early fifties. Carlos Kleiber was the first conductor I had ever worked with who took to heart Strauss's own suggestion, "Play it like Mendelssohn." Like his father before him, Carlos is one of those rare conductors who take the time to work with singers. No expression, no nuance, is left to chance. And he allows the voices to be heard. (Opera, after all, is song with orchestral accompaniment.) It was an indescribable pleasure to be able to sing all the *piani* and *pianissimi* that are marked in the score, instead of having to shriek every

note so as not to be drowned out by the *fortissimi* of a merciless orchestra. Moreover, it leaves more strength for the genuine crescendos and climaxes. I am glad I was able to meet and work with this brilliant conductor.

Above left: As Elektra at Covent Garden in 1968. Above: *Elektra* in 1977 with, from left to right, B.N., Carlos Kleiber, Gwyneth Jones (Chrysothemis), and Donald McIntyre (Orest).

Paris

It is hard to miss the Théâtre National de l'Opéra in Paris, for it looms up somewhat pretentiously in the very heart of the city. The building, a grandiose work by Charles Garnier, was opened in 1875. Kristina Nilsson—the Swedish soprano who was the prima donna of the Paris Opéra in the 1860s and 1870s—never performed there, however. And my own guest appearances in Paris, compared with those in other cities around the world, have been quite sporadic—a brief sojourn as Turandot, one as Isolde, and three visits to sing Elektra. The primary reason is that until the early 1970s the repertory, with a couple of notable exceptions—Wieland Wagner's *Tristan* and the lavish new production of *Turandot* in 1967–68—was terribly meager.

The *Turandot* was an orgy of costumes and scenery the likes of which I have never seen. There were about four hundred people on stage, counting singers, chorus, ballet, and extras. One critic wrote that even the Folies-Bergère seemed modest by comparison with the splendor displayed by the Paris Opéra in *Turandot*. After four extravagant performances, the chorus and orchestra went on strike, and *Turandot* was discontinued.

The former head of the Hamburg Opera, composer Rolf Liebermann, eventually became General Manager of the Paris Opéra. With his great charm and energy—and with enormous government subsidies—Liebermann managed to some extent to awaken the Opéra from its Sleeping Beauty trance. To the best of my knowledge, however, Liebermann never revived the incredible *Turandot*. I don't know why, but my guess is that the production was too lavishly praised *before* Liebermann became General Manager. And the same phenomenon is now being repeated under Liebermann's successor, Bernard Lefort. Rather than allow the public to go on enjoying the best productions from Liebermann's day, Mr. Lefort prefers to borrow productions from Angers, Trieste, and other places. It's what I'd call an extravagance of personal prestige!

Turandot in Paris.

Revolution in Buenos Aires

I arrived in the Argentine capital for the first time in 1955, just before Juan Perón was overthrown. I was to sing five Isoldes at the famous Teatro Colón, a stately and aristocratic hall, full of traditions and covered with enough patina to let you know you are dealing with a genuine theatre. The stage and the house are enormous, and I quickly discovered that in order to reach the audience I would have to alter my style and enlarge all my gestures. If raising an eyebrow had been sufficient in Stockholm, then to achieve the same effect here I would have to lift both arms above my head. But the acoustics are magnificent, and singing requires no more effort than in a much smaller theatre. Voices carry with amazing ease.

After two performances of *Tristan*, however, the revolution broke out. The whole city closed down, and there was talk of evacuation. Since a curfew was in effect, there was little to do but sit in our hotel room and play cards and hope for better times. The worst part was getting up and down stairs from the fourteenth floor, for of course the elevator operators were out on strike. One night my husband and I woke up to find the entire hotel shaking, and we heard repeated explosions.

Along toward morning we learned why. The news on Radio Montevideo reported that Peronista headquarters—in the next block to our hotel—had been destroyed by shellfire. Three hundred Peronistas had been killed, and an equal number had surrendered. Perón had fled to Montevideo during the night. The next day all was peaceful again, and after another day or two the performances at the Teatro Colón could be resumed. The public was giddy with joy, they cheered for the new president, for Wagner, even for Nilsson. In order to give the performances within the period stipulated in the contract, we had to sing *Tristan* three times in four days, a feat not to be recommended except in times of revolution . . .

In the midst of the shellfire I had sworn that if only I could get out alive, I would never again set foot in Argentina. But I went back the very next year, and several times since I have been the object of the wild and violent enthusiasm of the Argentines.

My fans often gathered at the airport outside Buenos Aires when I was due to arrive and greeted me with big Welcome banners. On my last visit, there were about a hundred of them. It was a warm reunion, naturally, with flowers and various demonstrations of affection, and the crush was almost unpleasant. When

I reached the hotel, I discovered that my jewelry and my money had been stolen. It had been the simplest thing in the world, of course, for a professional thief to mix with the crowd of enthusiastic admirers and open the zipper on my big shoulder bag. But it made my arrival in Buenos Aires pretty dismal—though my departure was all the more festive. After my final performance, the stage was heaped with flowers and I waded in roses literally up to my knees. I think the Argentines are the most passionate fans I have ever met; they are almost reckless in their affection.

In October 1967—in the midst of four complete *Rings*—I sang an orchestral concert at the Teatro Colón, arranged by the beautiful and energetic Señora Jeanette de Erize, left, President of the Mozarteum in Buenos Aires. On the right, Carina Ari di Moltzer, Swedish-born, a former ballerina, a sculptress, and a patron of the arts. She has lived in Buenos Aires for thirty years and was not only a popular member of the Swedish community but also a focal point in the artistic and social life of the city.

As the Marschallin in *Der Rosenkavalier*. Buenos Aires, 1956.

47

San Francisco

Standing peaceful and white on many hills, it is one of the most beautiful cities in the United States. The climate is marvelous, the temperature always just right. Most singers are very eager to sing in San Francisco. If you are there as early as September or October—the opera season lasts only about three months in the fall —you can spend much of your free time by the swimming pool. So perhaps General Director Kurt Herbert Adler, capable as he is, does not deserve all the credit for the fact that artists find the San Francisco Opera so attractive that they are willing to accept generally lower fees than in, say, Chicago, in order to sing there. Adler was in charge of the War Memorial Opera House when I first sang there, in 1956, and he still is. I have often said that anyone aspiring to be an operatic general manager should learn the job from Adler. He is not always the easiest man in the world to deal with, but what he has accomplished in San Francisco is worthy of the greatest admiration.

New York

Lincoln Center is an attractive and impressive place, with its Metropolitan Opera House flanked on one side by the New York State Theater and on the other by Avery Fisher Hall, as the home of the New York Philharmonic is now called. The façade of the Metropolitan, facing Lincoln Center Plaza, is very decorative. In the evenings, when the buildings are brightly lighted, the huge Chagall paintings in the upper foyer can be seen through the tall windows from outside and are strikingly effective.

On December 18, 1959, I was finally to make my Met debut— as Isolde—in the old opera house. I was not in a proper mood for the adventure. I guess I felt I had been neglected a little too long. After all, I was forty-one years old and had already made my mark at most of the leading opera houses around the world. I had sung at the San Francisco and Chicago Operas in 1956—to great acclaim. Rudolf Bing had heard me sing in Europe on a couple of occasions, without so much as a word. I almost felt that I had somehow "missed the boat."

After my debut, I realized how wrong I had been. I should instead have been grateful to Bing for ignoring me. For in the meantime I had developed and matured as an artist, and my debut

Whenever I wanted a change of air I would go up to the roof terrace of my residential hotel on Eighty-second Street. It also provided a splendid background for photographs, as in this picture, with half of New York at my feet.

was a critical and popular knockout, as the saying goes. Overnight I was first-page news in the big American newspapers and magazines. The critics wrote that a star had been born. No one seemed to realize that I had been a star for several years in Europe. Or was it that they thought that didn't count? And perhaps they weren't far wrong. Suddenly I understood. A singer can have one triumph after another in Vienna, Bayreuth, London, Milan, etc., and no one will pay a great deal of attention. But a similar success at the Met will echo through papers all over the world.

The period after my debut was incredibly hectic. All at once I was known all across the United States. Television, opera, concert, and recording companies swamped me with attractive offers. There were interviews and photographs from morning to night.

During the first two weeks, I never left the hotel except for performances. I had absolutely not a moment in which to enjoy my new fame, but it was nice to know that my fortune was made, and that I would be able to take things a little easier when I came back the following season. Or so I imagined. I discovered when I did return that these assumptions were utterly incorrect. No one recognized me on the street anymore, no one came up and asked me for my autograph, and even at the Met enthusiasm had dwindled considerably. I was no longer a sensation. It was like a slap in the face. So I sat down in my loneliness and started to reflect on my situation, and I arrived very quickly at the following solution to my problem: *work and more work*. In order to maintain my position, I would have to improve significantly. In my profession, standing still is a step backward. That second year at the Met was an instructive one for me, for I realized that while it may not be so awfully hard to reach the heights, it is very hard indeed to stay there.

My New York debut as Isolde was conducted by Karl Böhm, who also had one of his greatest American triumphs that evening —at the age of sixty-five! My Tristan was to be Ramón Vinay, a brilliant artist from Chile, who was already well known in Europe, particularly as Tristan and Otello. His tenor, which had a baritone quality, had by then begun to darken somewhat, and he was very nervous. He was indisposed for my debut and was replaced by German tenor Karl Liebl. Vinay sang the second performance but withdrew before the third. In Bing's day there were always lots of understudies at the Metropolitan, because to cancel a performance was financially catastrophic. These under-studies—sometimes as many as four for a single role—were called "covers." Since Wagnerian tenors don't exactly grow on trees, there were only two covers on the third occasion—and both of them declared themselves too ill to handle a role such as Tristan. But Bing was never at a loss. With his great charm and power of persuasion he got the three tenors to agree to sing one act apiece, and, as he explained to me, he saved the fattest one for last so I would have something soft to fall on in my "Liebestod" scene. The evening was saved! A swarm of photographers appeared at each intermission, and the performance was a sensation in all the newspapers, where it was spiced up with headlines such as: SWEDISH ISOLDE USES UP ONE TRISTAN PER ACT.

By the poster outside the old Metropolitan a day or so before my debut.

Isolde posing with her somewhat reluctant Tristans. Left to right: Ramón Vinay; first cover Karl Liebl, wearing his own overcoat while waiting to take over the costume from Vinay; second cover Alberto da Costa, wearing the third-act costume.

My very first performance in the United States was in Hollywood, in August 1956. Manager Wynn Roccamora heard me sing Salome on a radio broadcast from Stockholm and immediately offered me an engagement at the Hollywood Bowl. When I arrived in Los Angeles, a score of reporters and photographers were waiting at the airport. I looked over the other passengers trying to figure out who the press had come out to meet. There must be a movie star on the plane, I thought, but who was it? When it finally dawned on me that all the fuss was for me, I suddenly felt very ordinary in my simple cotton dress with its brightly colored pattern of glasses and straws.

For me, as for so many other first-time visitors, Los Angeles was a disappointment. The city lacked charm and appeal. The people, however, were tremendously friendly, helpful, and generous, and in no time at all I felt right at home in the movie capital. The Hollywood Bowl is an outdoor concert hall—only the stage is roofed—and actually resembles a gigantic basin, surrounded as it is by gentle hills. It will hold a good twenty-five thousand people. Concerts are amplified so that everyone can hear. It was a beautiful, warm evening, and I was almost giddy with happiness as I gazed out across the enormous sea of faces. Thanks to a big promotion campaign by Mr. Roccamora, nineteen thousand people had gathered for the Wagner concert.

Rudolf Bing, or Sir Rudolf, as he was called after being knighted by Queen Elizabeth, was very particular about getting contracts with his stars signed a quickly as possible. He did not much care for oral agreements and looked extremely skeptical when I told him there were opera houses with which my contracts were purely verbal. Once, after what he described as a sleepless night, he came to my hotel at ten in the morning to get my signature on a contract. For the sake of the publicity, a photographer was often called in to immortalize our latest covenant.

After more than twenty years as General Manager, Sir Rudolf was succeeded, to the amazement of many, by Göran Gentele from Sweden. His name was completely unknown to most Americans. A few people seemed to know that he had a very pretty wife, but that was about all they did know.

Those of us who had worked under him in Stockholm were tremendously eager to see whether he would be able to realize his artistic ambitions in a considerably larger opera house and in a foreign country.

Only a few weeks before he was to take over as General Manager at the Met, in September 1972, we received the crushing news that he had been killed in a traffic accident in Sardinia, along with two of his daughters. Mrs. Gentele and another daughter were injured but survived.

The heaviest obligation I ever fulfilled was to sing at their funeral. All our hearts went out to Marit Gentele when, with admirable self-control, she stepped forward into the chancel and said farewell to her loved ones in their three coffins.

The funeral at Ingarö Church in Sweden. On the left, Mr. George Moore, President of the Metropolitan Opera Board. Then B.N. and Mr. Schuyler Chapin, who was to have been Gentele's assistant manager but who now suddenly became General Manager himself. He is a very likable and pleasant man.

Several roles at the Met

Tristan und Isolde, Act I, 1959–60 season. To the left of Isolde, Irene Dalis as Brangäne. To the right, Karl Liebl, a tenor from Wiesbaden, as Tristan.

Salome, 1965. Salome is the only role I ever asked to sing at the Met. Bing took the risk and, in the same breath, promised me a new production. Karl Böhm conducted, and Günther Rennert was an inspiring director. The production was such a success that people in New York still talk about it. Jokanaan in this picture is William Dooley, the American bass-baritone.

Amelia in *Un Ballo in Maschera*, 1963, with the Swedish setting. Richard Tucker is Gustav III.

Die Walküre, 1965.

Lady Macbeth, 1964.

Elisabeth in *Tannhäuser*, 1966.

My "home" in New York

The Hotel Alden, at Eighty-third Street and Central Park West, where I always stayed, was for many years home to a number of Met artists. It lay within comfortable walking distance of the new Metropolitan, and right across the street was Central Park, New York's gigantic "lung."

At the Alden you could rent a furnished one-, two-, or three-room apartment with a kitchen, and a great many dinners and parties were given there. The hotel changed hands, unfortunately, and what with the slums pressing in on all sides, opera people began looking around for other places to stay. But I have a lot of pleasant memories from my fifteen seasons at the Alden.

Above: Three happy Graces: Regina Resnik, Joan Sutherland, and B.N. I have noticed, especially in New York, that people are very careful about inviting two or more prima donnas to the same party. Presumably they have had bad experiences of such constellations. But on the few occasions when I was invited somewhere along with other "stars" there was never any blood shed.

Regina Resnik began her career as a dramatic soprano but then moved into the mezzo category and became, to name just one example, an incomparable Klytemnestra in *Elektra*. The Australian *prima donna assoluta* Joan Sutherland, a coloratura soprano nonpareil, is a simple, unaffected woman. She had a hard time getting started, dreamed of becoming a Wagnerian soprano, and sang minor roles at Covent Garden until her husband, conductor Richard Bonynge—who was then a pianist—discovered that she could sing coloratura better than anyone else alive.

Carnegie Hall is a fantastic concert hall. Nowhere else is the concert atmosphere so taut, nowhere else is audience enthusiasm likely to burst out with such frenzy. The acoustics are perfect. Just to *give* a concert at Carnegie Hall is in some ways to succeed. This is the poster for my first concert there, in 1961.

Right: Signing autographs after *Aïda*. At the Met, on October 14, 1963, I sang Aïda in a new production. It was the season's Opening Night. Georg Solti conducted, Carlo Bergonzi—one of the world's leading tenors—sang Radames, and the American mezzo-soprano Irene Dalis sang Amneris. I had a serious gallstone attack the evening before and was awake all night, but after almost a month of intense rehearsal I thought it would be a terrible shame to miss the premiere. Somehow I managed, although I suppose I have given better performances.

Whenever someone had a birthday, all of us would rally round. Here Frau Thea Böhm's birthday is being celebrated by, from left to right, Leonie Rysanek, the famous soprano from Vienna; George London, a brilliant Don Giovanni, Scarpia, Wotan, etc.; Mrs. Böhm herself with her husband, Karl Böhm; me; and Jess Thomas, who eventually gave up his Italian repertoire to become a fulltime Wagnerian.

All the years I studied I dreamed of playing the role of Elisabeth in *Tannhäuser*. When I finally got the part, I felt I could not do it justice. I found that I was best suited for dramatic assignments rather than for characters with halos on their heads. The only times I have been even remotely satisfied with my interpretation of Elisabeth were those evenings when I was also allowed to play her antithesis, the wicked and seductive Venus. In some way this gives me a better perspective on Elisabeth. The first time I was persuaded to sing both female leads on the same evening was in

1966, at the Met. (Obviously, they do not appear on stage at the same time.) I was terribly nervous about trying to play these two very contrary characters in the same performance. But it worked better than I had expected. I discovered that the two roles breathe life into each other, and that it felt right that they should be sung by the same person. Later I also did a recording in which I sang both roles. The picture of me as Venus and as Elisabeth is, of course, a composite.

My comeback

In March 1975, I sang what I thought was my last performance at the Met. The Internal Revenue Service of the U. S. Government had demanded a sum of money in back taxes that I could not possibly pay. I felt I had no choice but to turn down further engagements in the United States. I was naturally very sad at the thought of never again seeing my dearest fans, and of having to part with them under such painful circumstances.

Four years passed. I was by no means unemployed, but I have to admit that hardly a day went by that I didn't miss my American public. We had grown very close during the sixteen years I appeared in the United States, and I had given them the best years of my career.

Then one fine day I got a letter from a man I had never heard of, an American attorney who declared himself to be a great admirer of my singing. He had missed me, he wrote, and he offered, at no obligation, to try and work out an agreement between me and the I.R.S. In other words, he wanted to help me negotiate a manageable schedule of payments. Imagine my amazement when, two months later, he had succeeded where three other lawyers, in the course of ten years, had failed. I could return to the United States!

Mr. Anthony Bliss, the Met's new General Manager, arranged an orchestral concert for November 4, 1979, with me as soloist to celebrate my comeback, no, call it rather my homecoming.

As long as I live I will never forget that evening. Four thousand people rose to their feet and let loose an ovation unlike anything I had ever heard. It felt as if those four thousand people were gathering me to their hearts one by one.

The orchestra played like angels. And James Levine! What a

conductor for voice! He literally read my intentions on my face and cushioned me with orchestral sound that made me feel as if I were floating on clouds. I love you, Jimmy!

And what of the attorney, you may ask. Well, Mr. Weissberger, a gentleman with a heart and good blue eyes, told me after the concert that it was one of the happiest days in his life, too.

Right: "It's a little bit of heaven on earth as the stars from the Metropolitan Opera ceiling meet up with star Birgit Nilsson as she studies a *Tosca* score in an orchestra seat. The Met has lowered its giant chandelier and is in the midst of cleaning it in preparation for the opening of its season, September 15, 1968." (U.P.I.)

Beverly Sills, *prima prima donna* and the declared darling of the American public, has many strings to her lyre. When she is not appearing in one of her brilliant roles, she is the energetic manager of the New York State Opera, or she is hard at work on some TV show, or, as here, she is interviewing another artist. Beverly becomes so intensely involved in her interviews that after a few minutes you forget the audience completely and are only conscious of being engaged in an extremely pleasant and relaxing tête-à-tête.

Lauren Bacall and I are not speaking sign language, as it might appear, but discussing and demonstrating vocal technique.

On November 27, 1967, I sang my one hundredth Brünnhilde in *Die Walküre*. The picture below was taken in my dressing room at the new Met with one hundred red roses. It was a new production of *Die Walküre*, directed and conducted by Herbert von Karajan, and everyone had been complaining about the dense gloom that prevailed on stage. On opening night I received an anonymous present—a miner's helmet with a lamp in front and Valkyrie wings on the sides. Whoever the anonymous donor may have been, the management seemed well informed, for just as I stood in front of the mirror trying out this new headgear, Sir Rudolf and two of his assistant managers appeared unexpectedly, all three of them with suspiciously mischievous glints in their eyes.

A distinguished visitor in my dressing room at the Met: Rosa Raisa, who sang Turandot at the world premiere at La Scala in 1926.

Julie Andrews, the original Eliza of *My Fair Lady*, is a warm and delightful person in private as well as on stage. Here we are backstage at the Met after a performance of *Turandot*. Left to right: the enchanting Mirella Freni; Julie Andrews; and the tenors' tenor, Franco Corelli, or, as he is called by Italian women, *cosce d'oro*—"golden thighs."

The 1971–72 season was to be Rudolf Bing's last at the Metropolitan, and in December 1970, Göran Gentele, then head of the Stockholm Opera, was named to succeed him. In the spring of 1972 there was a farewell concert for the departing General Manager—a gala evening that will long be remembered. Part of the concert was made into a recording and part of it was televised, and all the profits went to the Met, which has always had a tough time making ends meet. Sir Rudolf asked the Met's foremost artists to take part. The result was an exhibition of beautiful voices and fabulous attire that lasted into the small

hours. Bing asked me to sing the final scene from *Salome* and added that, for inspiration, he would give me his head on a silver platter. Since he is one of those rare people who can take a joke as well as make one, I told him it was quite unnecessary, I could use my imagination. Our little exchange was reported in the press, and, just in time for my entrance, a piece of sculpture representing Bing's head was delivered to me on a silver tray. The giver or givers were anonymous. There was great hilarity in my dressing room when Bing turned to Gentele and said, "There you see what becomes of General Managers at the Met!"

Twice I was invited to the White House. The first invitation was from President Lyndon Johnson and Lady Bird Johnson. I was in Europe at the time and could not accept. The second was an invitation to dinner from President Richard Nixon and his wife, Pat. I was to sing for a group of Argentine politicians, diplomats, and businessmen. Since I was to give a concert at the Kennedy Center in Washington on the following day, this invitation suited me perfectly. But when I discovered at the last moment that my accompanist, John Wustman, had had no invitation but was to take part only in the performance, I decided to skip the dinner myself and appear only for the concert. Mr. Nixon gave me a long, personal, and very knowledgeable introduction that he delivered without notes. He had the speech as well as the concert taped—as was his custom. A copy of the tape with a letter of thanks and the photograph above was sent to me. Several years later he sent me a copy of his memoirs with a very friendly and personal dedication.

To Birgit Nilsson
With admiration, appreciation and best wishes,
Pat Nixon
Richard Nixon

Farewell old Met!

On April 17, 1966, the old Metropolitan closed its doors forever at the conclusion of a gala concert. A great many people wept at the prospect of this Temple of Song, with its wealth of traditions, being leveled with the earth to make way for a gigantic steel-and-concrete office building. The Metropolitan Opera House had opened on October 22, 1883, with a performance of *Faust* in which my famous namesake, Kristina Nilsson, sang a brilliant Marguerite. Her many admirers presented her on that occasion with a laurel wreath of pure gold, and the well-known New York critic Irving Kolodin suggested that, as a Swede, I should wear this laurel wreath at the farewell concert for the building Kristina Nilsson had helped to dedicate. In her will, she left this treasure to the Music Museum in Stockholm, and the Museum, in a gesture of great trust and generosity, sent it to the Swedish Consulate General in New York. Here it is being entrusted to my care by then Consul General—now a retired ambassador and Master of Ceremonies of the Swedish Court—Tore Tallroth, who is at the same time admiring a present to me from my own admirers, a replica of the curtain at the old Met in the form of an enormous gold brooch.

To conclude the final, gala concert at the old Met, I sang the final scene from *Götterdämmerung*, at left.

The first thing I always did on arriving at the Alden Hotel in New York was to put up the Swedish flag.

This is what the Gramophone looked like sixty or seventy years ago. In those days, recordings were made by singing into a large funnel. A musical guessing game was arranged for one of the intermissions in a radio broadcast from the Met. Some of the leading music critics in the United States were invited to guess who the singer was on an old Gramophone cylinder. But in fact I had made the recording myself—on ancient equipment. It consisted of several bars from Sieglinde's role in *Die Walküre*, and none of the critics guessed it was I. One of them said that whoever the voice belonged to, she could never have been an important singer. Ever since, I have been more careful about criticizing artists on the basis of old recordings.

Taking bows after an evening of *Siegfried* at the Met. At the left is Erich Leinsdorf, a veteran at the Metropolitan, where he was already a conductor in Kirsten Flagstad's day. He is an extremely intelligent musician, and we have done a lot of performances and made a lot of recordings together over the years. On the right, the Austrian set designer Günther Schneider-Siemssen.

Singer Dorothy Collins presents me with a Grammy for the Nilsson-Tebaldi-Björling-Leinsdorf recording of *Turandot*. The prize, which is given by the National Academy of Recording Arts and Sciences, consists of a miniature Gramophone.

Curtain call at the Met after a performance of *Turandot*. The conductor is Zubin Mehta, the popular and talented Indian who succeeded Pierre Boulez as conductor of the New York Philharmonic.

I have sung in thirty-four of the fifty states of the Union, but since there are few opera companies in the United States, I have sung mostly concerts. Occasionally my local folk costume would find its way into my luggage. On such occasions I usually began by singing some Swedish folk songs, then changed into an evening gown for the Lieder portion of the concert. My accompanist in these pictures, John Wustman, is an American. We have worked together for twelve years, and he is an invaluable support and an excellent traveling companion. The latter quality is very important, for we are thrown into each other's company a great deal on these long and often exasperating journeys. These pictures were taken in Pittsburgh.

Welcome visitors in my dressing room after a performance of *Elektra* at the Met. From left to right: Marit and Göran Gentele, who had just been named the new General Manager at the Met; Peter Diggins, the Met's Assistant Artistic Administrator; and Geraldine Souvaine, who produces Texaco's Metropolitan radio broadcasts. During the performance—in the middle of the dance—I tore a muscle in my right leg. It was dreadfully painful, and I had to leave the stage on crutches. Gentele tried to comfort me. "Don't worry about a thing," he said. "They make absolutely terrific lightweight artificial limbs these days."

Christmas in New York.

My suite at the Alden Hotel was always called the flowershop by the maids. It may be that the quantity of flowers in the picture above is even greater than usual, however. A lot of people had heard of my accident and chose this delightful way of showing their sympathy.

The wonderful Mr. Arnold Weissberger, the lawyer who brought me back to the United States.

A quick lunch of "Birgit's meatballs" at the Alden.

Christmas Eve in New York. Karl Böhm with his two favorite singers, as he used to call us. On the right, Leonie Rysanek.

On March 4, 1974, I had a serious accident during a rehearsal at the Metropolitan. During the quick scene change in the first act of *Götterdämmerung*, the stagehands somehow failed to properly attach some steps leading to a raised platform. When I started to make my exit down these steps, they collapsed, and I fell with them. I landed hard and then discovered I couldn't move my right arm. Still in full Brünnhilde gear, I was taken to Roosevelt Hospital. My shoulder was dislocated, and I had to be anesthetized before they could put it back into place. My friends said it was a tragicomic sight to see me being rolled into the emergency room in long, false eyelashes, Brünnhilde's flowing red wig still on my head, and my face disfigured by cuts and bruises. The premiere of the new production of *Götterdämmerung* was only

four days off, and I simply couldn't bear the idea of not singing. By the morning of the day of the opening, my dreadful headache had almost disappeared, and I decided to go ahead with the performance. A cape was quickly sewn up—it had to cover my arm, which was lashed to my body. I will never forget the ovation when Jess Thomas and I made our entrance. A lump came to my throat, and I was close to tears. It took me several minutes to get control of myself. What a fantastic evening. The audience virtually held me up with their approval and good will. Several critics maintained that it was the best *Götterdämmerung* I had ever sung. But it was two years before I had the full use of my arm again.

Moscow . . .   . . . and Warsaw

My guest performances in Eastern Europe have been limited to two occasions. In the fall of 1964, La Scala was invited to give a series of performances in Moscow, and I was engaged to sing four Turandots, two at the Bolshoi and two in the gigantic Palace of Congresses inside the walls of the Kremlin. The ensemble —soloists, chorus, orchestra, and ballet—consisted of 449 Italians and one Swede. The performances were more or less reserved for politicians, party bigwigs, and other privileged types, so we never got a chance to sing for the genuinely interested musical public or the common people. The Bolshoi Theatre has atmosphere and fine acoustics. The dressing rooms are very homey, with geraniums in the windows and rag rugs on the floors. The Palace of Congresses is very modern. The performance is piped into the dressing rooms on closed-circuit television. The house has fifty rows of seats and can accommodate six thousand people. For opera, the place is quite impossible. The performers have no contact with the audience, and the acoustics are virtually nonexistent. All performances make use of a German amplification system that includes a hundred and thirty microphones concealed on stage.

In May 1975, I sang a single performance of *Tosca* in Warsaw in what is said to be Europe's most modern and, at least in terms of sheer cubic meters, largest opera house. The house was almost completely destroyed during the war but was reopened—much of the original façade preserved—in 1965. The applause was so tremendous that I was more than happy to repeat "Vissi d'arte," a thing I had only done a couple of times before.

Rehearsing with the
Sydney Symphony
Orchestra and Sir
Charles Mackerras.

Sydney

In 1973, after ten years of toil, the opera house in Sydney was finally to be dedicated. After concerts in Perth, Adelaide, and Melbourne, I arrived in Sydney, a city of skyscrapers crowded together along quite narrow streets. Surrounded by these enormous buildings, a pedestrian can easily feel oppressed. The theatre and concert hall, however, is charmingly situated on the open tip of a narrow promontory and is in perfect harmony with its surroundings. On the outside it resembles an enormous sailing ship, and looking out a dressing-room window you might think you were on a great Atlantic liner. The architect was Danish, and the unique white tile plates that cover the sail-like roofs were specially ordered from a factory in Höganäs, near my home. But the interior does not quite measure up to the lavish exterior, and it is very clear that a different architect with less imagination and more limited financial resources completed the decor. In addition

to a couple of smaller concert halls and theatres, the building contains a main concert hall with a capacity of 2,700, done completely in lilac, and an opera house all in black that will hold an audience of about 1,500. I was soloist with the Sydney Symphony Orchestra at the opening concert in the large hall. Sir Charles Mackerras, an Australian well known in Europe and the United States, conducted, and, because the building had cost several million dollars over its original budget, he asked me to begin the concert with Elisabeth's song of greeting from *Tannhäuser*, "Dich teure Halle" . . . I sang two other concerts as well, an orchestral concert with the Cleveland Symphony Orchestra, Lorin Maazel conducting, and an evening of Lieder with the extraordinary Geoffrey Parsons—also an Australian—as my accompanist.

One of the last photographs ever taken of Fritz Busch. Full of honor and renown, he enjoys a quiet, relaxing moment with his wife, Grethel.

Above: Wagner conductor number one, Hans Knappertsbusch. He had an authority and a power over orchestras that was rare. He was no lover of rehearsals, but when, in performance, he stood up before the orchestra—and he was over six feet tall—he achieved results that other conductors, despite weeks of rehearsal, never approached. His broad tempi never seemed slow because his music was so emotionally charged, so full of skillfully fashioned surges of intensity. Still today there are Wagner conductors who attempt, usually in vain, to imitate Knappertsbusch by conducting slowly. To them I would give the same advice I always want to give boring public speakers: "If you've nothing in particular to say, then at least say it quickly!"

A *Salome* rehearsal in Munich, 1955, with Joseph Keilberth, left, a perfect conductor for singers, and Rudolf Hartmann, director and at that time head of the Bavarian State Opera. Hartmann also directed my first *Elektra*, in Stockholm in 1965.

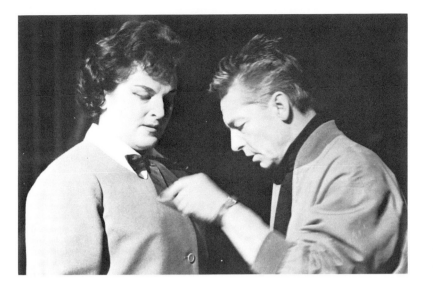

Anatomy lesson from Herbert von Karajan: "Now let's take the whole thing one more time, but this time with heart. The heart, Miss Nilsson, is located in here where you have your cashbox." Whereupon Miss Nilsson replied: "Why, then we have something in common, Mr. von Karajan!"

Opposite: My third "Comeback" Concert was in San Francisco, November 18, 1979. On the podium was Kurt Herbert Adler, who now holds the record as longest reigning operatic general manager—almost thirty years. He was inspired! The audience was the most enthusiastic I have ever seen in San Francisco.

Above: *Turandot* rehearsal in 1961 with Leopold Stokowski, center, then almost eighty, who was making his Metropolitan Opera debut! Left to right: B.N.; Mr. Trucco, the coach; director Nathaniel Merrill; Stokowski; Anna Moffo, who sang Liù; and Franco Corelli, Calaf.

A cheerful discussion during an *Elektra* rehearsal in Hamburg. In the middle, August Everding, director and General Manager of the opera there. On the right, Leonie Rysanek, a wonderful friend and an incomparable Chrysothemis.

Some encouraging words before a performance of *Turandot* in Munich from the late Günther Rennert, General Manager of the Bavarian State Opera and an able director. I have had the privilege of working with him on *Salome* at the Met, *Elektra* at La Scala, and the *Ring* in Munich.

Below: The end of a *Salome* concert in Chicago with Sir Georg Solti conducting. Beside me, Ruth Hesse, who sang Herodias.

Left: An attempt to do away with a rival. Ingrid Bjoner is Norwegian, a wonderful singer and colleague. She was playing Isolde in Munich, and here I am giving her a big hug. She knows how to be magnanimous, however. She has a new car, a SAAB, that she has christened Birgit, with the name painted in large letters on the door.

A few of many caricatures

"You haven't really made it until you've been in *Playboy*," someone has said. The honor was vouchsafed to me when *Playboy* published this caricature. The artist was inspired, presumably, by the severe winter in New York.

This drawing of me as Salome is from a book of caricatures of famous musicians published in Germany.

After a mishap at the Met during a dress rehearsal of *Götterdämmerung* in 1974—I dislocated my arm but sang on opening night despite the injury—this cartoon accompanied Alan Rich's review in *New York* magazine. I was given the original as a present.

The drawing on page 7 was done by Einar Nerman, who has become famous for his telling caricatures of celebrities in the world of cinema, theatre, and music.

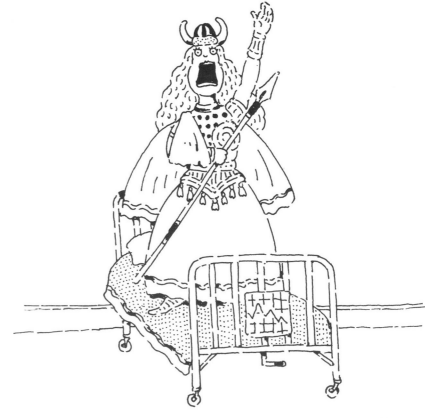

At right: One of the first international Swedish tenors I sang with was Torsten Ralf. After the war—since his prewar home in Dresden had been destroyed—he settled in Stockholm, and in the early fifties he made frequent guest appearances at the Stockholm Opera. I worked with him in *Tannhäuser, Lohengrin, Die Walküre, Tosca,* and *Aïda.* Like me, he was a native of Skåne. He was a pleasant, self-assured man, built like a singer with a good-sized head and a powerful throat. The resonance of his head was fantastic, and his voice rang beautifully from his forehead. I began to understand that here lay much of the secret of a singing career. On the left, Anders Näslund, still wearing Telramund's armor and makeup.

After a performance of *Tristan* in Barcelona, 1958. Three Swedes dominated the ensemble: second from left, Kerstin Meyer, singing Brangäne for the first time; in the middle, B.N.; second from right, Erik Sundquist, who sang Kurvenal. The man in tails is the East German conductor Franz Konwitschny, head of the legendary Gewandhaus orchestra in Leipzig. Between him and B.N. is Wolfgang Windgassen, who sang Tristan. I was presented on this occasion with the gold medal of the Gran Teatro del Liceo, which had previously been awarded only to a very few Spanish-born singers.

Between two of the world's foremost tenors, Jussi Björling and Set Svanholm. The place is the well-known Drei Husaren restaurant in Vienna. Earlier that year—1960—I had been honored by King Gustaf VI Adolf with the *Litteris et artibus* medal but had been unable to return to Sweden to receive it. Set Svanholm, who was then General Manager of the Stockholm Opera and had come to Vienna to sing at the Musikverein, brought the medal with him. Jussi was in Vienna to make a recording, and I was singing Brünnhilde in *Götterdämmerung* at the Vienna State Opera. We celebrated the informal presentation of the medal with a good dinner, topped off patriotically with Swedish pancakes and lingonberry jam.

Left: Three "generations" of Swedish Brünnhildes in one picture, 1977. B.N.; Irma Björck, who was legendary in the 1930s and '40s; and Berìt Lindholm, who was superb when we alternated in the part in Bayreuth and at the Met and in Chicago.

Center and below: Two fantastic Swedish singers who are warmly and actively remembered, especially by the musical public in America. Center photo, Karin Branzell in New York, with her husband, Fedja Reinhagen. Karin was a delightful person who took genuine pleasure in the success of younger colleagues. She never missed an important event at the Metropolitan. We became very good friends.

Below, seated, Kerstin Thorborg, backstage at the Liseberg Concert Hall in Gothenburg, sometime in the late 1940s. I met her only once—we sang in the same concert—but I remember her as a warm person and an extremely dramatic artist.

Below: Swedes invade the Metropolitan. It was March 1975, and bitterly cold. The entire *Ring of the Nibelungen* was performed several times at the Met with Sixten Ehrling conducting. Sixten is not in the photograph because he stayed inside for fear of catching cold, but the Swedish singers took the risk and posed in the pale March sun. Left to right: Ragnar Ulfung (Mime), B.N., Bengt Rundgren (Hunding and Hagen), Kolbjörn Höiseth (Loge and Siegmund), and Berit Lindholm (Brünnhilde). I alternated that year between Brünnhilde and Sieglinde.

WITH THE STOCKHOLM OPERA ABROAD

When I was a Resident Artist with the Royal Swedish Opera I naturally took part in their guest appearances abroad. In later years, too, I always found it pleasant to join old friends and colleagues when the Opera traveled. Here is a handful of pictures from such trips.

Wiesbaden, 1955

We gave a guest performance of *Die Walküre* at the International Drama Festival in the provincial capital of Hesse. Left to right: Set Svanholm (Siegmund)—he became General Manager of the Stockholm Opera the following year—B.N. (Brünnhilde), Sigurd Björling (Wotan), Sixten Ehrling, and, on the right, Sven Nilsson (Hunding), a cousin of my father's. Everyone in this picture has since had his own success at the Met.

Montreal, 1967

The Royal Swedish Opera opened a series of guest performances by Europe's leading opera companies at the Universal and International Exhibition in Montreal—Expo '67. I came straight from the Met's spring tour, and I sang Isolde. In this picture we are leaving Montreal after the final performance. Left to right: Josianne Varviso, Silvio Varviso, B.N., Göran Gentele, and Rolf Leandersson. A glimpse of Göran Gentele's wife, Marit, can be seen over his right shoulder. I went back to Montreal with the Vienna State Opera several months later, toward the end of Expo '67, and sang an *Elektra* and an orchestral concert.

Edinburgh, 1974

When the Opera went to Edinburgh in 1974, I sang Elektra twice. Sweden's ambassador in London, Ole Jödal, had a large reception after the opening-night performance, and among the guests was Ingrid Bergman, who had come to Edinburgh with her husband, Lars Schmidt, especially for our visit.

What is actually the difference between a fan and an opera lover? Real fans are opera enthusiasts who concentrate all their attention on one particular artist. Fans will often come from another country or another continent—traveling as cheaply as possible on hard-earned money, laboriously saved—to be present at an event where their idol is performing. True fans will defend even a bad performance tooth and nail, for in their eyes their heroes and heroines are paragons. Greater loyalty does not exist. They live vicariously, somehow, through the artist, and are at the same time thoroughly unselfish. They have great respect for a singer's profession and never intrude unnecessarily. They know that in order to perform really well, a singer must be able to work in peace. I have many of these wonderful fans, and I cannot imagine what a career would be like without them.

Above left: After a performance of *Un Ballo in Maschera* in Stockholm in 1960, I was given a special tribute by the "gallery" and was then carried from the stage in a golden chair.

Left: A "fan party" at our house on Lidingö, just outside Stockholm. On either side of me, children of a former colleague, tenor Conny Söderström. On the left, Leif, now a well-known opera director, and on the right, his sister Gunilla, now an opera singer.

With some of my most ardent fans after a concert in Gothenburg in 1979. Left to right: Gunnar Olsson, a Swedish fan who almost never misses a performance, whether in Europe or the United States; Birthe Bernfeld, an equally well-traveled Danish fan; Dorothy Sivertson of Pasadena, California, my very first American fan (1954); Gordon Salter of San Francisco, in a T-shirt that reads "Brava Birgit Goddess Divina Assoluta"; B.N.; Ulla Jonsson, another Swedish fan of long standing (1963) and extensive travels; Liselott Franneck, from West Germany; and Nickey Silvey from New Orleans, wearing the same T-shirt.

77

WITH MY FANS

Among my fans I must count Denmark's Minister of Culture, the late Niels Matthiasen. Niels, who was a great opera and ballet lover and a cheerful, charming, and loyal friend, has fallen at my feet during a supper at the home of the Swedish press attaché in Copenhagen, Benkt Jerneck, now Swedish Consul General in Berlin.

Welcome visitors in my dressing room at the old Met after a performance of *Aïda* in 1963: Swedish Foreign Minister Torsten Nilsson, and Sweden's Ambassador to the United Nations Agda Rössel.

Extremely intense idol worship can lead to displays like the one on this young doctor's wall.

With royalty

In March 1979, the Swedish royal couple made an official visit to West Germany, the first since Miss Silvia Sommerlath of Heidelberg became Queen of Sweden. They visited Munich, among other cities, where Carl XVI Gustaf first met Miss Sommerlath and where, by his own account, something went "click" the moment he saw her. She was a hostess at the Olympic games and had been assigned to act as the King's guide.

The Munich Opera now gave a performance of *Elektra* in their honor, with me in the title role. The audience was a collection of distinguished representatives of the cultural and political life of both Sweden and West Germany.

This is not usually the most appreciative kind of audience. Many of them are there because they have to be, others go in order to be seen in the right places, and such affairs are often stiff and uninspiring.

This particular evening, however, was a marked exception to the rule. I have seldom experienced a more genuine and spontaneous enthusiasm. The magazine *Oper und Konzert* said of it, "The exit of the exalted guests caused less of a stir than their entrance, incidentally. In the meantime, the public had chosen another queen, Birgit Nilsson, the Unsurpassed."

After the gala performance of *Elektra*, Dr. Franz Josef Strauss, the Minister President of Bavaria, gave a supper for about a hundred guests. Above, left to right: Carl XVI Gustaf, B.N., and Queen Silvia.

Right: After a concert in Monte Carlo I was invited to supper with Prince Rainier and Princess Grace of Monaco.

The Begum, Princess Aga Khan, has always been a loyal opera lover. Here she visits me in my dressing room after a performance of *Elektra* at Covent Garden in London.

I have performed in Oslo only once, many years ago. King Olav was present. In November 1975, he came to Stockholm to pay a state visit to our young king, Carl XVI Gustaf. As I was staying in Stockholm at the time, preparing a new role—as the Dyer's Wife in *Die Frau ohne Schatten*—I was asked to perform at the traditional gala in his honor at the Opera. A few days before the concert I was made a Knight Commander First Class of the Order of St. Olav. This is Norway's only order, and is said to be awarded very sparingly. The First Class decoration consists of two large stars, which I am wearing on my concert gown beneath the Order of Vasa, First Class. It was a happy and genial King Olav who received me during an intermission in the performance.

Recording sessions are among the worst ordeals I know. It takes a long time to make friends, as it were, with the microphone, which is cold and demanding but extremely sensitive. After a few retakes, you can fall completely into its power. All you care about is feeding this uninspiring lump of metal with technically perfect tones, forgetting all about feeling and expression. And so then all you can do is go back and start from the beginning. In the picture at the left, I am making a brave attempt to put some intensity into my singing. It was taken in Prague during a recording of *Don Giovanni* with Karl Böhm.

Above: Listening to a recording of *Tristan* made during an actual performance in Bayreuth, a method that I personally prefer. Left to right: Wolfgang Windgassen (Tristan), Eberhard Wächter (Kurvenal), B.N., Martti Talvela (Marke), and a technician from Deutsche Grammophon. Left center: To judge by our expressions, a successful take. Left to right: John Culshaw, the Decca producer; B.N.; and conductor Edward Downes. The picture was taken in London. Lower left: As I travel I am occasionally asked to autograph my records in a record store. This normally draws quite a crowd of autograph hunters, and the record store does a good business, we hope. Here in New York, Franco Corelli and I are signing our *Turandot* recording.

fact often ignored by conductors and hence by orchestras and singers as well. There are often complaints about the dearth of Wagnerian singers today. I believe that if conductors would better accommodate themselves to the singers they have, and that if they would pay more attention to Wagner's musical notations, then not only would we have more Wagnerian singers but also more great Wagnerian conductors.

During the spring season at the Metropolitan in 1975, I was to sing not only Brünnhilde in the *Ring* but also several Sieglindes in *Die Walküre*. Sieglinde is a role I have always loved, but I had not sung it since 1957 in Bayreuth, and it is no exaggeration to say that I was very excited about this "new" part. Sixten Ehrling conducted, and he was a rock I could cling to in my opening-night nervousness. Fortunately I also had Jon Vickers (left) as my Siegmund. He was an inspiring partner, and we were a huge success. In their enthusiasm, people tore their programs into small pieces and threw them from the balconies like confetti, and they broke the rules to throw flowers onto the stage.

Another trick picture (below), of me as Brünnhilde and as my half sister Sieglinde. As opposed to Venus and Elisabeth in *Tannhäuser*, these two roles cannot be sung by the same singer on the same evening, for they appear on stage simultaneously in a couple of scenes. When I sang my first Sieglinde at the Met, Berit Lindholm was a young and radiant Brünnhilde.

On Wagner, song, and singers

Laymen often associate the term Wagnerian with voices that are notable chiefly for their strength and that are not suited to other kinds of music. Nothing could be further from the truth. A Wagnerian with good technique should also be able to sing Italian opera. The famous soprano Lilli Lehmann, for example, sang everything from Brünnhilde to Norma, and on her sixtieth birthday amused herself by singing *La Traviata!* And Wolfgang Windgassen—Bayreuth's Siegfried and Tristan in the fifties and sixties—now and then sang other roles, such as Tamino in *The Magic Flute*.

Naturally a Wagnerian singer has to be equipped with a good physique and a certain vocal power in order to get through a performance lasting four or five hours and to be heard above an often heavily instrumented orchestra. But even if Wagner's style is unique, his music must nevertheless be sung *bel canto* just like the Italian classics.

Close study of a Wagner score will turn up a great many subdued notations in both the vocal and the instrumental parts, a

Senta

Senta in *The Flying Dutchman*, at the Lyric Opera of Chicago. This has never been one of my favorite roles. When I come to the phrase "Ich bin ein Kind und weiss nicht was ich singe," I am always afraid that the audience will burst out laughing. I guess I have never been able to portray childish naïveté convincingly!

It is sometimes asserted that Wagner has a special effect on the voice. One might go so far as to say that he sometimes seems to have a special effect on the profile too . . .

Richard Wagner. Sculpture by Arno Breker in the park outside the Festspielhaus in Bayreuth.

Brünnhilde in Wolfgang Wagner's production, Bayreuth, 1960.

Brünnhilde

In the course of an entire *Ring of the Nibelungen*, a Brünnhilde must cover quite an emotional range, from the all-wise, bravely fighting Brünnhilde of *Die Walküre* to the ardent woman awakened to love by Siegfried in *Siegfried*. The tremendous joy of Siegfried and Brünnhilde's love culminates in a duet that often leaves the singers as well as the audience breathless: "Himmlisches Wissen stürmt mir dahin, Jauchzen der Liebe jagt es davon." For Brünnhilde, this final duet ends with a high C that is much feared and was often transposed to a lower octave by earlier Brünnhildes.

Of the three roles, the Brünnhilde of *Götterdämmerung* is the most extraordinary. Aside from the fact that the part is longer than the Brünnhildes of *Die Walküre* and *Siegfried* put together, it also embraces the broadest dramatic and musical register. This Brünnhilde is still, in the Prologue, a young woman in love, but in the second act she is a woman betrayed, crushed, a vengeful woman who in her fury reveals Siegfried's vulnerability and resolves upon his death. In the third act she is once again the all-wise daughter of a god, resigned to fate, who, on her faithful horse, Grane, mounts the pyre where her hero is being consumed. Valhalla goes up in flames, the Rhine regains its ring, the curse of the gold is lifted, and a new and better world awaits.

Vocally, this role demands a broader range than *Die Walküre* or *Siegfried*. The middle register and the deeper notes have occasionally given me concern when dealing with an insensitive orchestra. But once I reach the last act's "Starke Scheite," such

trifles are forgotten. For then all one's resources are offered up on the altar of music in order to realize this most brilliant creation of the musical drama—the final scene of *Götterdämmerung*.

Above: A scene from the second act of *Die Walküre* at La Scala, 1958. The role of Wotan, Brünnhilde's father, is being played here by Hans Hotter. Above left: Brünnhilde in *Die Walküre* in Munich, 1969. Below: Brünnhilde in *Siegfried*, 1976—also in Munich, but in a different production.

Isolde

Isolde is a character of great complexity. However hard she strives, no actress can ever capture more than a few of the many colors on her palette. Still I think I can say that each of my 208 performances of Isolde—so far—has in some way differed from all the others. I love the first act where she tells Brangäne her deepest secret—how hurt she has been in her love for Tristan—followed by her meeting with Tristan himself, in which every phrase she utters is so full of hidden meaning that it can be sung in many different ways and always be right. It is often one's own mood that determines whether, at a given instant, hate or sarcasm, vengefulness or resignation, will lie closer to the surface. Only one thing is essential—that even in her most heated moments the audience must clearly sense the powerful undercurrent of her love for Tristan.

Vocally, Isolde is a wonderful role. The music is so splendid that one can hardly fail. Because it is considerably longer than any other part I have sung, however, it demands a great deal of strength and stamina.

Right: Isolde at the Metropolitan, 1959. Above: Isolde in Stockholm, 1966.

I have played opposite many wonderful Tristans. I sang more than eighty performances with Wolfgang Windgassen, and we knew each other and worked together so well that nothing was left to chance. Jess Thomas is another fine Tristan, with the looks to go with the part. We sang together in the recent, highly esteemed production at the Met, directed by August Everding and conducted by Erich Leinsdorf. Jon Vickers has given the part a personal touch and intensity that are all his own. Helge Brilioth, with his superb phrasing and clarity of expression, is a joy to listen to.

A pretty picture of the love duet from a guest appearance in Copenhagen in 1973. My Tristan here is Helge Brilioth. Notice the crisscrossed ropes in the background. They give the illusion of a sailing vessel but they also represent the bars of a prison. After all, the ship is carrying Isolde to King Marke in Cornwall, whom she is to marry against her will. The production was directed and designed by Peter Windgassen, the son of Wolfgang Windgassen.

One hundred roses for one hundred Isoldes. Bayreuth, 1963.

Two hundred roses for two hundred Isoldes. Vienna, 1976.

B.N. and Jess Thomas at the Met in 1971.

The final scene, Munich, 1976, with Dietrich Fischer-Dieskau, a wonderful Barak.

It was many years before I could be persuaded to take the role of the Dyer's Wife in Richard Strauss's *Die Frau ohne Schatten*, a work of great complexity from every point of view. Earlier, perhaps, the part of the Empress, with its high *tessitura* and its dazzling costumes, might have been more to my liking. But in retrospect I can see clearly that I made the right choice. For one thing, the Dyer's Wife is undeniably the more interesting of the two roles. For another, I had never before portrayed a simple, ordinary woman with commonplace problems.

While learning the part, my self-confidence sank virtually to nil, and I was very close to giving up. Not only does it cover a range of more than two and a half octaves, but, with its varying tempi and difficult intervals, the part struck me as simply unsingable, and the piano rehearsals left me hoarse and exhausted. Nor

The Dyer's Wife in

Die Frau ohne Schatten

Nikolaus Lehnhoff trying to change my mind, Stockholm, 1975.

Vienna, 1977.

could I take my distress to Richard Strauss as did the first Dyer's Wife, Lotte Lehmann, when she wanted to resign from the role. (Strauss himself took her under his wing.) But with the great support of Berislav Klobučar and director Nikolaus Lehnhoff I eventually changed my mind. And then when I finally began to sing the part with an orchestra, all the problems suddenly vanished into thin air. My voice carried through all the difficulties as if borne on wings.

The performances in Stockholm were a huge success for everyone involved. I have since sung the part in Munich, Frankfurt, Vienna, Hamburg, Berlin, Buenos Aires, and San Francisco and it has actually become one of my favorite assignments.

The *Frau* ensemble in Vienna, still unsurpassed. From left to right: Ruth Hesse (Die Amme), Walter Berry (Barak), Leonie Rysanek (Die Kaiserin), James King (Der Kaiser), B.N. (Die Färberin, i.e., the Dyer's Wife).

The set for the Dyer's house designed by Günther Schneider-Siemssen for the Vienna State Opera in 1977.

Elektra

Elektra in Berlin, 1977. My first guest appearance at the Deutsche Oper in ten years. A huge ovation—fifty-nine curtain calls!

Elektra

is a role I had been warned about all my life. Among other things, I was told that a singer who undertook this "voice-killing" part would be shortening her career by several years. And so I dutifully waited until 1965 before taking it on. I soon found that all the warnings had been greatly exaggerated. The part suited me perfectly. Elektra is no "screech role" as I had been led to believe. After a few dramatic outbursts in the first scenes, the rest of the part can be sung quite lyrically and with a slender tone. The role is taxing, of course, for Elektra never leaves the stage once she is on and she is musically active throughout the rest of the opera. But what a magnificent singing and acting part it is! Next to Isolde and Brünnhilde, it has become something of a favorite of mine, and, in spite of my rather late debut in the part, I have sung it on most of the principal operatic stages of the world.

My first *Elektra* rehearsal, Stockholm, 1965. Left to right: Berislav Klobučar, who conducted my first *Elektra* at my request; Rudolf Hartmann, General Manager of the Bavarian State Opera in Munich, who directed the production; Silvio Varviso, Musical Director of the Stockholm Opera; and Göran Gentele, Stockholm's General Manager.

Left: Gwyneth Jones sang Chrysothemis beautifully when I played Elektra at Covent Garden in May 1977.

Opposite: Elektra in her outburst of hatred for her mother, Klytemnestra, in Wieland Wagner's 1965 production in Vienna.

(More *Elektra* pictures on page 44.)

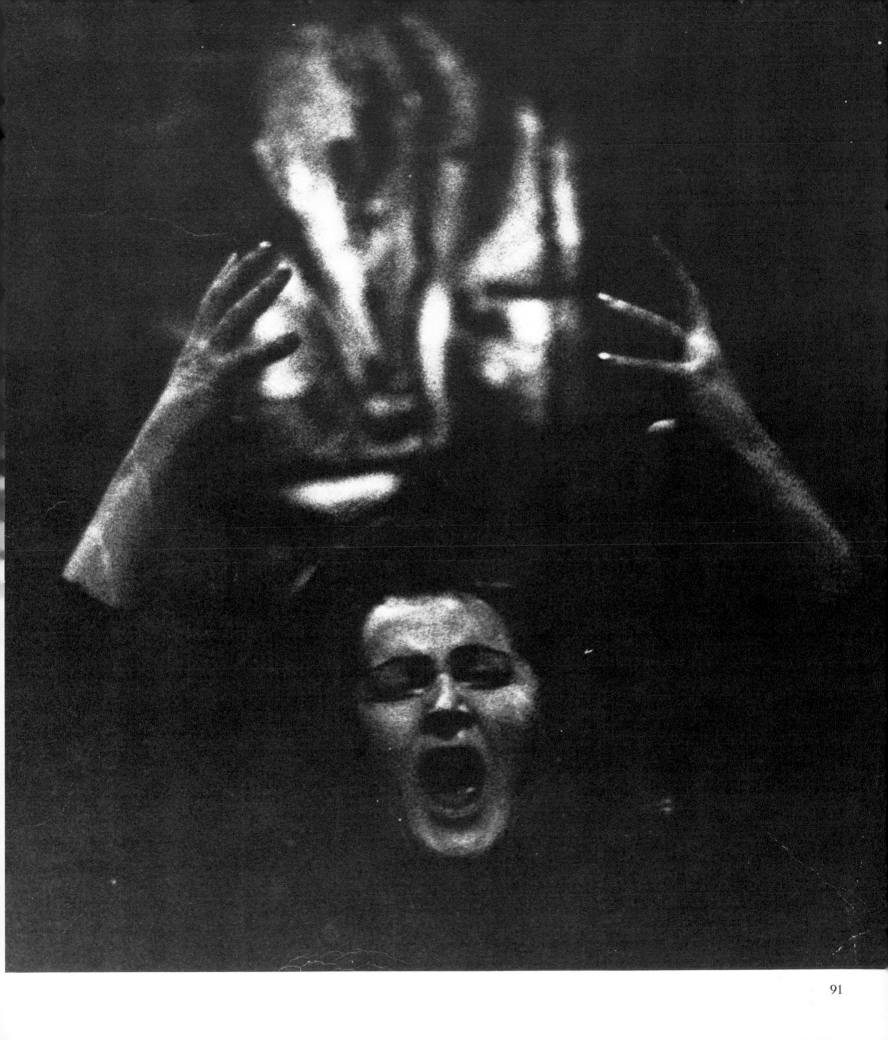

In Nicaragua I was flattened into a postage stamp as Turandot.

Turandot

Turandot in the Arena in Macerata, Italy, 1970, with Franco Corelli as Calaf.

Opposite: *Turandot* at the Metropolitan Opera House, 1961. The sets and costumes were designed by Cecil Beaton.

Despite the fact that it is relatively short by comparison with, say, Isolde, there is no other role in my repertoire as hazardous for the voice as Turandot. I feel almost like a trapeze artist before every performance—never really certain if I will land on my feet or my head. A single small technical mistake could do permanent vocal injury. I use a special vocal technique for Turandot, and I warm up for the part very carefully so that musculature, support, vocal cords, and resonance will function together perfectly. The difficulty with Turandot is that most of the role is written up around high C. After several demanding high notes, most opera composers will let the voice come down and rest for a time in a more comfortable range. Not so in *Turandot*. In order to adequately convey Turandot's emotional frigidity, Puccini quite deliberately lets the voice remain at these stratospheric altitudes, at times almost naked, accompanied only by a few fragile, "Oriental" tones.

As an acting assignment, Turandot is quite uninteresting. Placed far upstage at the head of a long flight of stairs, usually with an enormous train and an equally huge and heavy princessly crown, Turandot has little to do but give vent to her loathing for the men who, several thousand years before, captured and killed her ancestral mother (and therefore no man shall ever possess Turandot).

Why, then, should anyone want to sing so difficult and dramatically uninteresting a role? Vocally, I regard it as a challenge. I hold the world's record several times over for number of *Turandot* performances, and for the last fifteen to twenty years I have had the part pretty much to myself, at least on the major operatic stages.

Below: I sang Turandot in the great amphitheatre in Verona, Italy, in 1969. In the same cast was Placido Domingo, who was singing his very first Calaf.

Tosca

For most lyric-dramatic sopranos, Tosca is probably first on the list of desired roles. It means pretty clothes, jewels, and a chance to play a celebrated and pampered prima donna.

In my travels I have seen many performances of *Tosca*, and what so often amazes me is that even sopranos with reputations as fine actresses concentrate more on Tosca the diva than on Tosca the human being. It seems to me that what is primary is the woman in love, not the operatic leading lady. It is, after all, for the sake of love that she commits murder.

I don't know how Sarah Bernhardt played the part in Sardou's play—which vanished from the theatrical repertory with the appearance of Puccini's opera—but I am almost certain that even if theatrical prima donnas were enormously glorified in 1887, when the part was written for her, she nevertheless found space for Tosca the human being in her interpretation of the role.

I have played opposite many famous tenors in the role of Cavaradossi. One of the first was Beniamino Gigli (above left), who, with his sixty-two years, was perhaps more of a kindly uncle than a fiery lover. But how he sang! His voice was as supple as a rubber thread. From a *pianissimo* it could swell to a mighty *forte* and then soften again to a whisper.

Jussi Björling (left) had a voice no less beautiful than Gigli's. His singing style was utterly Italian, but he had that special timbre in his voice that no non-Scandinavian possesses.

Franco Corelli (above) was a handsome, virile Cavaradossi, and as Tosca I was no doubt envied by every woman in the theatre. But I have played opposite many a famous and inspiring tenor in the part, including Placido Domingo, Giuseppe di Stefano, Ferruccio Tagliavini and Franco Tagliavini, Carlo Bergonzi, Gianni Raimondi, James King, José Carreras, and such Swedish tenors as Ragnar Ulfung, Jussi's son Rolf Björling, Jonny Blanc, and others.

Scarpia: "And what of the fan, Tosca?"
Tosca: "I was jealous as usual."

S: "So Attavanti was not at the villa?"
T: "No, Mario was alone."

T: "Shorten his suffering! What do you mean?"

"It is thus that Tosca kisses."

"You shall strangle on your own blood."

"Die, you villain, die!"

"He is dead, he is forgiven."

"And before him all of Rome once trembled."

The Scarpia in these pictures is the Italian baritone Anselmo Colzani. The photographs were taken at the Metropolitan during an actual performance.

Fidelio—Beethoven's only opera

I sang my first Leonore in *Fidelio* in the summer of 1953 at the Bad Hersfeld Festival in West Germany. What a wonderful role and what splendid music! But Beethoven did not make things easy for voices. I am thinking particularly of the soprano parts in *Missa Solemnis*, the *Ninth Symphony*, and *Fidelio*, his only opera. Long passages of all three were written in a very high and uncomfortable range. Perhaps Beethoven's increasing deafness contributed to his lack of sympathy for the human voice.

Were it not for the great dramatic soprano aria "Abscheulicher, wo eilst du hin!"—one of the greatest arias in all opera—the role could well be sung by a more lyric soprano. As the part is written, the dramatic voice must reduce its weight considerably in certain ensembles and occasionally perform short coloratura passages.

New York, 1966.

At the Met, 1960, with Jon Vickers.

I have been criticized several times—perhaps primarily in England—for playing the first act in too cold and reserved a manner, in other words, for being insufficiently emotional. But I wonder if these critics have ever really considered Fidelio's situation. Disguised as a man and using the alias Fidelio, Leonore has gone into service at a government prison outside Seville. She hopes to find and rescue her husband, Florestan, a Spanish nobleman who has been missing for two years. Leonore plays the part so well that the jailer's daughter, believing her to be a man, falls in love with her. The situation is extremely dangerous. The slightest suspicion by the prison governor, Pizarro, could mean death for her and Florestan. Therefore I find it extremely important to play the part with reserve—right up to the moment that Leonore falls into the arms of her liberated husband. I have no intention of altering this interpretation of the role.

97

Salome

Once I got Salome under my skin, as it were, she became one of my favorite roles. The part is not as long as Elektra, and perhaps not as demanding either, in purely vocal terms. On the other hand, Salome has to perform a dance that lasts twelve minutes, a lot to ask when one stops to think that a solo for a prima ballerina lasts, usually, only three to five minutes. What Richard Strauss had in mind was a sixteen-year-old with the voice of an Isolde, and miracles of that kind don't grow on trees. Salomes are generally divided into two categories—those who sing the music superbly and those who dance the dance superbly. I don't suppose it is necessary to point out which category I fall into . . .

From a performance televised by the BBC in London.

Above right: New York, 1965.

Salome at the Met, 1965. Salome is in ecstasy over the severed head of Jokanaan. Irene Dalis is Herodias and Karl Liebl Herodes.

Lady Macbeth

who is power-hungry, to be sure, but who is also an exceptional coward—lets himself be talked into committing all those murders for the crown of Scotland.

To do the role musical justice, one would need three different voices—alto, dramatic soprano, and coloratura. In Vienna and Munich, moreover, the part is made even harder by having only one intermission instead of three. This means that, without any time to shift gears, one must leap fearlessly from the profound "La luce langue" to the merry coloratura of the banquet scene. The sleepwalking scene is of course a singing and acting *tour de force*. And, after all these breakneck vocal exploits, the next to last note that Lady Macbeth sings is a high D flat that Verdi has marked *pppp*.

Below: The sleepwalking scene at La Scala, 1964, directed by Frenchman Jean Vilar. Above left: The same scene in Vienna, 1970. Below left: The banquet scene at the Metropolitan, 1964.

My second role at the Royal Opera in Stockholm was as Lady Macbeth in Verdi's opera on October 10, 1947. Since my first operatic performance—as Agathe in *Der Freischütz* one year earlier—was an unprepared, last-minute substitution, I regard Lady Macbeth as my actual debut. Of course the role was much, much too difficult for an inexperienced singer, but nevertheless I was deliriously happy each time I got to play the part.

Lady Macbeth, a fountainhead of evil, cruelty, and ambition—what a part to sing and act! My feeling is that Lady Macbeth must exercise an incredible erotic power over her husband. Otherwise, it is almost impossible to comprehend why Macbeth—

Aïda

I sang my first *Aïda* in the spring of 1951 at the Stockholm Opera, where I have sung most of my roles for the first time. Fritz Busch conducted. Afterward he admitted that it had been his first *Aïda* too.

For a Wagnerian dramatic soprano, Verdi is technically more difficult than Puccini. His shadings and phrasings are considerably more subtle. In order to make it clear that he really wanted a note sung softly, Verdi often doubled and sometimes even tripled his *pianissimo* markings—one can even find such indications as *pppppp*. Such notations make a real impression on singers with an overabundance of power and energy who are used to singing a bold *forte*. With this role I began to restrain my vocal enthusiasm and to learn the difficult art of subtlety.

Of course the second act finale—the Triumphal Scene—in which Aïda can drown out soloists, chorus, and orchestra with her high C, is my cheapest victory, but then, too, my *pianissimo* high B and high C began to find favor with audiences and critics. This new technical refinement stood me in good stead later in my career. I think it would be salutary for most Wagnerian sopranos to sing an Aïda every now and then just for the sake of vocal control. But unfortunately there are not many today who are willing to make the effort.

Two photographs of *Aïda* at the Metropolitan in 1963. Below: A scene from the first act, with Carlo Bergonzi as Radames, Irene Dalis as Amneris, and B.N. Left: The Triumphal Scene, with Mario Sereni as Amonasro.

Amelia in Un Ballo in Maschera

I sang Amelia in *Un Ballo in Maschera* for the first time in the fall of 1958. The place was Vienna, and the cast has perhaps never been surpassed. Giulietta Simionato sang Ulrica, Giuseppe di Stefano sang Riccardo, and Ettore Bastianini sang Renato, while Dmitri Mitropoulos conducted. I had to polish Verdi's *cantilenas* very hard indeed to make myself noticed in that company.

Since, despite its Italian names and Boston setting, the opera actually deals with the assassination of a Swedish king—Gustav III —at a masquerade ball in Stockholm in 1792, the opera is a popular feature of the Stockholm repertory. In 1958 I began learning a new translation by the distinguished Swedish poet Erik Lindegren, a member of the Swedish Academy and thus one of

the men who choose the winners of the Nobel Prize in Literature. I discovered that Lindegren's text, however brilliant in itself, had the effect of chopping the musical phrasings to bits. Verdi often extended a single word over several beats in order to achieve the legato he desired. But Lindegren did not hesitate to alter the value of Verdi's notes, to cut up whole notes, say, into smaller ones in order to pack in as much Swedish history and literature as he possibly could.

I was at a loss about what to do and wrote a letter to Set Svanholm, who was then General Manager in Stockholm, complaining of my predicament. I stressed that I could not serve two masters and that undeniably I found Mr. Verdi more important than Mr. Lindegren. Svanholm, who was anxious to have me

participate in the Stockholm Opera's guest performances of *Un Ballo in Maschera* in Edinburgh in 1959 and in London the following year, gave me permission to alter or delete those parts of the libretto that I found musically unworkable. It seemed to me that I dealt with the text as cautiously as possible, but naturally Lindegren noticed what he called my "meddling." There was a supper after the first performance in Edinburgh, and in the course of it Lindegren began to give me a dressing down the likes of which I had never heard before, or since. I got up from the table and left the restaurant, but if I thought that Lindegren would give up that easily, I deceived myself. He pursued me out into the street and halfway to my hotel, subjecting me to a hail-storm of insults and abuse. Later, when he had calmed down, he

Opposite: An exclusive concert on the stage of the Stockholm Opera with my father as the entire audience. The picture was taken in December 1966.

wrote me a letter and apologized. But naturally I have held my Swedish Amelias to a minimum.

In the Swedish production directed by Göran Gentele, Gustav III was portrayed as an effeminate, self-centered gentleman who only pretended to be in love with Amelia. This made Amelia look a silly goose, of course, for failing to notice how much more interested Gustav was in his page than he was in her. Obviously Verdi did not picture the relationship between the King and Amelia on this platonic level when he composed the opera. In their love duet on Gallows Hill, the music practically glows with passion. Ragnar Ulfung gave a fantastic performance in the Gentele production, even though I cannot help feeling that that whole version was in conflict with Verdi's music.

Left: The final scene of the second act at the Vienna State Opera, Ettore Bastianini as Renato.

Above: Amelia at the Metropolitan, 1963.

Thirtieth anniversary

All those years at the Stockholm Opera! Where did they go? It seems like yesterday that I sat on that stage with trembling hands and knees, sewing Agathe's bridal linen in *Der Freischütz*. D Day (for Debut) was October 9, 1946. J Day (for Jubilee) was exactly three decades later.

By my own wish, I celebrated the thirtieth anniversary of my debut at the Royal Swedish Opera with a performance of *Tristan und Isolde*.

I had a cold, a runny nose, a husky throat—but you can't cancel on your "birthday."

Jubilee dinner at Operakällaren restaurant with colleagues, friends, supporters, and "gallery" fans—the most loyal kind. Some had come all the way from New York. My companion at dinner was my old friend Niels Matthiasen, Denmark's Minister of Culture, who, in a speech that drew cheers, said he couldn't understand why the Swedes needed nuclear power since, after all, "they've got Birgit!" On the left, Roland Pålsson, chairman of the Opera's board of directors.

A big crowd of reporters and photographers at the obligatory press reception in the Royal Foyer at the Stockholm Opera. Ylva Bokstedt, daughter of General Manager Bertil Bokstedt, had ordered an enormous cake with the inscription "Birgit 30 Years." Oh, if only it were true!

Roses and more roses . . . none of them with thorns. Congratulatory speeches, fanfares, presents. Every speaker mentioned only my good points—it was almost like being at one's own funeral.

The Nobel Prizes

In 1968 the Nobel Committee asked me to sing at the Nobel Prize Award Ceremony at the Stockholm Concert Hall. It was quite an experience to be present on such an occasion, and I felt greatly honored at being allowed to take part. The whole royal family was on hand—King Gustaf VI Adolf, Princess Sibylla, Crown Prince Carl Gustaf, Princess Margareta of Denmark, Prince Bertil, Princess Christina. In the first row, the 1968 Nobel Prize winners. Left to right: Luis W. Alvarez (Physics), Lars Onsager (Chemistry), Robert W. Holley and Har Ghobind Khorana (Medicine), and, on the far right, the winner for Literature, Yasunari Kawabata. In the second row I recognize several previous Nobel Prize winners: Ragnar Granit, Hugo Theorell, and Arne Tiselius; Professor Carl-Gustaf Bernhard; and a couple of members of the Swedish Academy: Lars Gyllensten and Eyvind Johnson.

My dear friend Johannes Norrby, chairman of the Concert Society for almost thirty years, has missed hardly one of my concerts in Stockholm since the first time he heard me sing, at Jakob's Church in 1942. He was also the first person to engage me for a large public concert—at the Stockholm Concert Hall in 1945.

Skansen

The City of Stockholm has an outdoor museum of old farms and buildings called Skansen, where, toward the end of May 1977, a complete farmhouse from my home province of Skåne was opened and dedicated. An earlier Skåne farmhouse had burned down some years ago, and now a charming old farm complex built around a central courtyard had been moved from the parish of Kävlinge and reassembled in the open-air museum. The festivities went on for seven days, with Skåne handicrafts and folk music and folk dances and more, and every evening there were appearances by "native" artists. On the evening of the dedication itself, the place was packed. King Carl Gustaf was there, along with a host of dignitaries from Stockholm as well as Skåne. Enthusiasm ran high, the speeches were numerous and not particularly brief, and the temperature—near freezing—was not allowed to dampen our high spirits. I paid for it later with a bad cold that kept me in bed for a week and forced me to cancel several foreign engagements. But I had been there the week that Skåne came to Skansen.

Love affair of the year at Tivoli

The annual concert at Stockholm's Gröna Lund has its traditional counterpart at Copenhagen's Tivoli. I hope I will be forgiven for quoting an article in *Berlingske Tidende*, a Copenhagen daily, the day after my concert there on August 4, 1977:

"What the super pop stars couldn't manage was accomplished by fifty-nine-year-old Miss Nilsson from Svenstad in Skåne. Without amplification, merely with vocal cords that must be made of iron rails, she turned Thursday evening at the Tivoli Concert Hall into the Concert of the Year. A passionate love affair developed between 'La Nilsson,' the great operatic prima donna, and an otherwise aloof Scandinavian public, which threw its reserve to the winds and abandoned itself to total adulation. The annual Tivoli concert with Birgit Nilsson is sublime art—but it is something more, a combination religious ceremony and exuberant folk festival that begins at the moment she makes her sweeping entrance, enveloping the first violinists in chiffon, and doesn't end until, an hour and a half later, we stand on our chairs and cheer like Mediterranean opera fans."

As for the love affair, it is highly mutual! The little Danish soldier in the bearskin cap is a grandchild of conductor Eifred Eckart-Hansen.

After the dedication of the farm, several of us were transported to the outdoor theatre at Skansen in a haycart. On the right, King Carl XVI Gustaf.

Gröna Lund

It has been a tradition for more than twenty years that I give an annual concert at Gröna Lund's Tivoli, the amusement park in Stockholm. The weather gods are usually merciful, and sometimes the crowd numbers in the tens of thousands. It is wonderful to sing for so large and so appreciative an audience, and I eagerly look forward to these concerts.

In 1979 I had the honor of being cast in precious metal for Copenhagen's Tivoli. When Niels Jorgen Kaiser became its manager, he decided to give a Tivoli Medal every year. This was the fourth. The artist was the Swedish sculptor Rune Karlzon.

Gothenburg

The people of Gothenburg went all out for the celebration of their city's 350th anniversary in 1971. Among other things, they sponsored a production of *Aïda* in their gigantic new sports arena, the Scandinavium. Soloists, chorus, orchestra, ballet, extras, everything functioned perfectly under the direction of Leif Söderström and the baton of Sixten Ehrling. A splendid production, to compete with the one in Verona. There were three sell-out performances with a combined audience of 25,000, plus 3,000 at the dress rehearsal. At an extra performance, Aïda was sung by an as yet unknown Helena Döse, and she became famous over-night. What opera enthusiasm there is in Gothenburg! The city really deserves a new opera house.

I happened to mention in an interview that the stage of the Scandinavium was so enormous we really needed roller skates to get around. The next day, a motor-driven scooter was placed at my disposal.

Garbo

Several summers ago, Greta Garbo was the houseguest of our friends Count Carl-Johan Bernadotte—the uncle of our king—and his wife Kerstin. One day they called and invited us over for dinner. We were the only guests, and we were urged to come early because Gigi, as they called Garbo, goes to bed with the chickens. I had a case of nerves like an opening night at the prospect of meeting the divine Garbo.

Rarely if ever has anyone made such a strong impression on me. She was radiant, with an almost unbelievable inner beauty. Still, I think it was her voice that I found most captivating. I don't remember what she said. As far as I was concerned, she could have read from the telephone book—I would have been equally enraptured. Her voice was a beautiful symphony of soft and melancholy tones. We enjoyed each other's company, and at eleven-thirty—long after the chickens were asleep—she waved us goodbye on the front steps. Before we left, she expressed a desire to attend my concert in Copenhagen a few days later. And she did come, together with her host and hostess. Unfortunately, a photographer recognized her during the intermission and she was frightened and saddened at never being left in peace.

During the intermission at a concert at Tivoli in Copenhagen. Left to right: my husband, Countess Bernadotte, Greta Garbo, and the well-known interior decorator Björn Thulin.

My Tosca wig gets a finishing touch from Inga-Britt Mengarelli while Gunvor, our right-hand woman, gives a final glance at Tosca's gown.

Backstage

Perhaps not everyone who is "uninitiated" understands how very important it is for performers to have first-class assistance behind the scenes with costumes, makeup, and wigs. A poorly dressed wig can spoil an entire performance. Once, at Covent Garden, my wig actually fell off in the midst of an opening night. I wept with rage. The next day a critic wrote, "The wig let her down but fortunately not her voice." Negligence in such matters irritates me terribly. But it cannot be easy for dressers and hairdressers to deal with nervous and demanding artists. They never get to stand in the spotlight, and no one in the audience gives a thought to whether or not they have done their work well. Therefore I think it is all the more important that we performers show our assistants the appreciation they deserve and that we understand fully how essential they are to a good performance.

The personnel in Stockholm are superb. One has perfect confidence that nothing will be left to chance. I always arrive two hours before curtain time, and Gunvor Wennerström is already there. She sees to it that all hooks and eyes are in place. She produces a prettier tiara or a lace handkerchief as if by magic and makes last-minute alterations if the costume has become too large or too small since the last time it was worn. She unwraps flowers and writes on each card the kind of flowers that were sent. She serves coffee or tea. In short, she does everything for everyone and is balsam to our nerves.

Putting on my Aïda makeup
in my dressing room.

A last glance in my dressing-room mirror.

Naturally there are splendid staff people abroad as well. At the Metropolitan there is a fantastic hairdresser, Nina Lawson, whom I worship. Good dressers are harder to find, even though the Met usually supplies two of them. Often buttons are missing, or one finds that a hem that came out at the last performance has not been mended. And if you should ask for a cup of something hot to drink, they look at you as if you had lost your mind. At the Met, you have to bring your own electric element.

In Vienna and in Germany, the staff is usually first class. In Milan, Paris, Buenos Aires—in the Latin countries, in other words—you are well advised to take a quick course in wig-dressing, for you will get little or no help from the so-called hairdressers, whose ineptitude makes them merely an annoyance.

The wonderful Nina Lawson preparing my hair for my entrance as Elektra on February 1, 1980—my first operatic role at the Met in five years.

Tired but happy after a *Tosca* performance in Stockholm. All my mascots are in place. I won't enumerate them all, but there is my cat, Petrus, who was given to me on the opening night of *Macbeth* in 1947, and my bull, Curlytop, who has crossed the Atlantic several times, and a monkey who is my comfort in moments of doubt—you wind her up and she applauds.

111

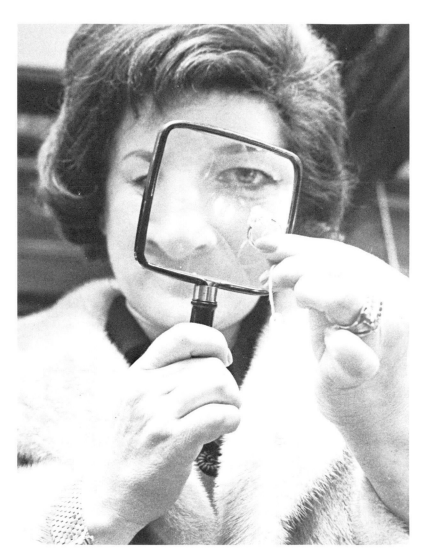

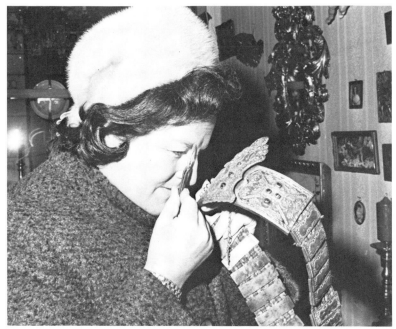

A magnificent antique Russian belt, set with precious stones. It would look wonderful on, say, Elisabeth's costume in *Tannhäuser!*

Admiring a beautiful ring in Vienna. (It doesn't cost anything to look . . .)

At an auction display at the Dorotheum in Vienna.

Hobbies

I am sometimes asked what my hobbies are—since I sing only in the evenings and have my days free. My usual reply is that if they had my working hours, most people would probably quit their jobs immediately. There are endless preparations and details that must be attended to—programs and clothing have to be planned, and there are rehearsals, costume fittings, photographs, interviews, negotiations, packing and unpacking, traveling, letter writing, telephoning and telephoning and more telephoning. Dealing with people—friendly and not so friendly. They all have one thing in common, however—they steal minutes or hours of your life. If on top of all this you have several homes to take care of "in your spare time," well, then, sometimes you have the feeling that the most restful hours you spend are the ones spent on the opera or the concert stage.

To tell the truth, it was many years before I began to look on singing as a job. My reasoning was that a job simply *cannot* be this much fun. Therefore I can say that one of my hobbies is . . . singing.

When in London or Vienna, I often make myself "unavailable" and stroll out to an auction or an antique store. Both cities are hazardous to work habits, however, because there are new auctions every day. Much the same is true in Buenos Aires. Once when I was sitting at an auction in Buenos Aires waiting for an item I very much wanted to acquire, a man came up and simply

stared at me. "But, good Lord," he said, "aren't you going to sing Isolde in a couple of hours?"

I always travel with a *loupe* or a magnifying glass in my pocket. It is a very practical thing to have if you want to take a closer look at a stone or a piece of jewelry. Moreover, the dealers take you more seriously. It never hurts to give the owner of the shop the impression that you know what you're doing.

If you want to meet foreigners in London, the place to go is the antique market on the Portobello Road. One of the first people I saw there one morning was Bertil Hagman, Press Director of the Stockholm Opera. He was looking for what is called a tantalus—a small liquor cabinet from Queen Victoria's day which usually consists of three crystal decanters that can be locked ingeniously into the case that holds them. He said he dreamed of setting out such a tantalus on the table, gesturing toward the three full bottles of liquor, asking his guests to help themselves, and then discovering at the last moment that he has lost the key. Hagman is known for being a careful man, and no price could be agreed upon. So there was no tantalus—that day.

The trick at such markets is to haggle and bargain for all you're worth, and the dealers expect it. Once during some tough negotiations in Camden Passage, the dealer suddenly said to me, "Madame, you haggle almost as well as you sing!" She got her price without another word.

On my birthday three years ago, some of my Swedish fans gave me a very pretty antique rocking chair. With it came a white crocheted shawl, a hymnal, a pair of granny glasses, and an old handbag containing the start of a knitted stocking. It was the highlight of the day, and I thought the hint was charming. Unfortunately, or, rather, luckily enough, I haven't yet had time to finish knitting the stocking.

I have a unique and beautiful collection of dolls made by clever, artistic admirers in Sweden and the United States. Above, the Swedish doll collection. The largest doll, in the rear, is of Brünnhilde in *Die Walküre*, equipped with helmet, spear, and shield, just like the actual armor I wore in 1955, as the picture above left shows. The smaller dolls too are wearing exact copies of costumes I wore at the Stockholm Opera in the 1950s. In the front row, left to right, are Brünnhilde, Tosca, Penelope, Turandot, Isolde, Fidelio, and Salome. In my hands I am holding Donna Anna, Isolde, Turandot (Act III), and Senta.

The dolls in the lower photographs—I have more that are not pictured here—are perhaps even more unusual. They are carved from some soft wood, and all bear a remarkable resemblance to me. They are dressed in precise copies of costumes I wore at the Metropolitan. Each figure has been placed in half the shell of a goose egg, which has then been framed with pearls, rhinestones, and colored stones. They are fantastic little works of art. The woman who made them and gave them to me is named Helen Kraybill and lives just outside New York. She is a very artistic woman and spends much of her time directing plays and making costumes. From left to right, below: B.N. dressed for the final gala concert at the old Met, wearing Kristina Nilsson's golden laurel wreath; Turandot; Fidelio in a defensive stance; and, finally, the double role of Venus and Elisabeth in *Tannhäuser*.

My father and I having lunch at Operakällaren restaurant in Stockholm in the fall of 1966. The food was so good he wondered if the whole kitchen staff had been imported from Skåne. The chief pastry cook, Hugo Hedberg (who does come from Skåne, naturally) had concocted an involved and seductively delicious dessert that he called "Peaches Birgit Nilsson." In return, I am giving him my autograph.

Several of my record jackets include, among my vocal merits and exploits, the sentence "She is also a very good cook." This is probably something of an exaggeration. The truth is, rather, that my taste buds are well developed, and consequently I know how food is supposed to taste. In countries where the art of cooking is at a primitive stage of development, therefore, I prefer to do my own. Pure self-defense, in other words. In countries like France or Italy, it would never occur to me to touch a pot.

Cookbooks are not my favorite reading. When I do glance at one, I never follow the recipes down to the letter. Instead, I indulge a lot of my own whims and fancies, and the finished product differs considerably from the original, but it's more fun that way, and sometimes better.

My little kitchen at the Alden Hotel in New York. I am trying to throw together something edible for a few select friends I've invited to supper.

Christmas at Svenstad, the home of my parents, with what we call "lots of food and tasty food and food at the right time."

The duck pond at home.

Jenny Lind and I

One summer day five years ago we found three motherless kittens in a hollow linden tree. The mother had been run over by a car, and the kittens were about ten days old. I nursed them with milk from a doll's baby bottle. We named them Janne, Julia, and Jenny (Lind—Swedish for linden, of course). Jenny had a particular need for affection, and used to nurse on my earlobe. It's a habit she still has, despite being eight years old, although now it's my husband's earlobe she likes best. She adores 1) perfume, 2) mentholated cough drops, and 3) my singing. Whenever I practice, she clings to me and becomes terribly affectionate. So I have to schedule my practicing with her in mind. When she's out, I can sing. The whole household revolves around Jenny, and she knows it very well.

After ten months inhaling and exhaling theatre dust and one's own and other people's bacilli, it is pure wonderful to get outdoors and do something with your hands. Hedge-clipping is a fun but strenuous job. The worst part is the next day when you start to get stiff and sore.

The Heritage Society

When I was a child, my parents taught me to love and cherish the things our forefathers had created, and I developed an early interest in the history and traditions of our village. When the Bjäre Heritage Society was formed, my father was one of the first to join and contributed quite a large share of his collection of local relics and antiquities. So it was perfectly natural that as soon as I had the opportunity I began to do what I could to help the Society with its shaky finances.

Folk dancing on Midsummer Eve beside the timber houses of Palma farm. My father's mother was born in this very building, though at that time it stood in another village—called Pâarp—in West Karup parish. In the 1930s the farm was moved to the Heritage Society's land in Boarp and rebuilt there in its original form.

Every now and then I give a benefit concert for the Heritage Society. The first money I ever raised this way was used for a new thatched roof at Boarp.

In the course of my summer vacations, my father and I (right) would sometimes go for a ride in the small carriage to have a look at the crops. The excursion always ended on Svenstad's highest hill, the Judges' Ring (see below). The view is magnificent. To the southwest you can see Kullaberg and the waters of Skälder Bay. Straight west is the Kattegat. And toward the northeast there is Laholm Bay and the coast of Halland in the distance.

The Bjäre peninsula is beautiful, and to me it grows lovelier every year.

Between Tristan and Isolde. Tristan is always impatient until he's had his obligatory sugar cubes.

Nalle, an enormous St. Bernard, guards the house in Svenstad. He is so strong that I hardly dare approach him. He could knock me to the ground in sheer joy and enthusiasm.

More recently, the concerts have been held in West Karup Church. With a lot of good planning and good will, we usually manage to squeeze in about seven hundred people. The concerts normally take place at the beginning of July, when Mother Nature is at her most beautiful, and the weather is usually perfect. There is a very special atmosphere inside the church, which sparkles with candles and magnificent bouquets of flowers. A hand-woven rug, lent by its famous designer, Märta Måås-Fjätterström, covers the podium. Once again, the members of the Society have spared no effort. The combined choirs of West Karup and Båstad churches stand ready to take their pitch, and I feel a little extra solemn and thrilled at the opportunity to stand here before so many dear, familiar faces. It was here, after all, that I sang my first uncertain notes. I was a member of the church choir for eight years, and sometimes they even let me sing solos. The audience shows its appreciation by quietly rising to its feet after each section of the program, and I feel waves of affection and good will. It's good to be home.

Concerts at home

For many years I have given benefit concerts for the Bjäre Heritage Society. I derive a great deal of satisfaction from being able to lend a helping hand to the preservation of traditions, buildings, and artifacts from the area where my family has lived for so many generations and where I was born and spent my childhood and youth.

The first concerts were held in the Båstad church in 1955 and 1956 and brought in very modest sums of money. To the people of Bjäre, I was not yet famous enough. A few years later, tourists began making pilgrimages to the concerts, and now, recently, even the local people have begun standing in line for tickets. I guess there really is some truth to the old proverb about the prophet in his own country . . .

The photographs on the opposite page were taken during a concert at the Vegeholm Ice Stadium. Before finally deciding to hold the concerts in West Karup Church, we tried several other locations. The Båstad Tennis Stadium, for example, held a large audience, but the weather gods were not gracious, rain poured down, and all one could see of the audience were shawls and umbrellas. In 1967 the concert was moved to Vegeholm. It has space enough for a large audience, but the necessary alterations were cumbersome and time-consuming. Moreover, for reasons that are not so hard to understand, it is simply impossible to create the proper atmosphere in a sports arena, whether it is in Vegeholm, Gothenburg, or Lexington, Kentucky.

The concert at West Karup Church on July 7, 1979. At the piano, the talented Swedish pianist Lars Roos, who in recent years has accompanied me not only all across Europe but also in Teheran, Japan, and Korea. He is also a successful concert pianist and gave a much noted recital in New York in November 1979. For the concerts in West Karup, I managed to arrange tickets for five American fans who came all the way to Sweden just to hear them. The concerts were recorded, which explains all the microphones.

The makeup case

My most indispensable piece of luggage is my makeup case, which for many years accompanied me faithfully on all my journeys. It was an old fiberboard box, the kind that railroad men used to carry provisions in. I bought it in Stockholm in 1956 for twenty crowns, and in order to conceal its humble origins I covered it with hotel stickers from all over the world. I was very attached to this "mascot" of mine, and thought with horror of the possibility that it would not last as long as my vocal cords. I even used to tell myself and my friends that I couldn't sing without it. But in 1968 it suffered an irreversible decline and a new one had to be acquired. Everything must pass. But no other makeup case will ever be the same . . .

Vacation is over, my makeup case is packed again, and, as Brünnhilde sings in the first act of *Götterdämmerung*, "Zu neuen Taten!" ("To new deeds!")

INDEX

124

Photo Credits

Alfa Foto, Buenos Aires, 47; Hacke Anderson, Helsingborg, 112 left; Anderssons Foto, Vaxholm, 78 bottom; Angel Records, New York, 92; Arena di Verona, 93 bottom; Jacques Aubin, Paris, 45 top; Erich Auerbach, London, 42 top

R. P. Bauer: *Im Konzertsaal karikiert,* 1959, 73 top left; Fred Bayer, Vienna, 39 bottom; Bayreuther Festspiele, 28; Beth Bergman, New York, 63 bottom right, 66, 82, 97; Michael Brannäs/Kamerabild, 79; Ilse Buhs, Bayreuth, 23 left; Dennis Burke, Vienna, 74 bottom; Christina Burton, London, 43, 44 right

Eugene Cook, New York, 100

Dagens Bild, 75 top left (Harry Berger), 76 bottom right (S. A. Öström); Erika Davidson, New York, 35, 75 bottom right; Decca, 81 top left and middle left; Dominic, London, 98 top left and bottom; Charly Dutoit, Bern, 95 bottom

Stern Eklundh, Båstad, 117 top; Lars Falck, Halmstad, 119; Fayer, Vienna, 36, 37, 38 top left and right, 40, 88 bottom, 99 top, 103 left, front jacket photo; G. Felici, Rome, 33 top; Fox Photos, London, 18 bottom left, 42 bottom; Cato Franzén, 110 top, 120

Antony di Gesù, New York, 56; Henry Grossman, New York, 58 top left; Bertil Hagman, 78 top left; Charles Hammarsten, 52, 80 bottom, 106 bottom; Harnesk, Ystad, 14 bottom right; Hausmann, Vienna, 31 top; Kjell Hedlund, 80 left; J. Heffernan, 57 top and bottom right, 110 bottom; Hanna Hulla, Vienna, 88 top

Sven Järlås, 13 bottom, 16 top

W. Kane, Bayreuth, 26 bottom; Hans Karlsson, Förslöv, 117 bottom; Kehlet, 15 top; Rolf Klänge, 2; Jürgen Kranich, Berlin, 89; K. G. Kristoffersson, 41, 45 bottom, 48, 64 bottom right, 65 top, 104 bottom left; Kungliga Teatern, Stockholm, 17 top; Kary Lasch, 55 bottom, 101; Siegfried Lauterwasser, Bayreuth, 21 bottom, 22 top, 23 middle and right, 24, 25, 26 top, 27, 81 right

Angus McBean, London, 18 top; Mélançon, New York, 50 top, 51 left, 58 bottom, 59 bottom, 60, 71 bottom, 86 bottom left, 94, 95 right, 98 top right, 103 right; Robert Messick for San Francisco Opera, 70 bottom right; Raoul Morichetti, Macerata, 93 top; Eleanor Morrison, New York, 54 top; Rigmor Mydtskov-Steen, Rønne, 86 top right

Einar Nerman, 7; New York Magazine, New York, 1974, 73 bottom left; Nordisk Pressefoto, Copenhagen, 106 top, 109

Oberfränkischer Ansichtsverlag, 21 top, 83 right; Oefyw-Markowitsch, Vienna, 34

Kristian Pahlmark, 114 bottom; O. Palffy, Vienna, 87 right; Piccagliani, Milan, 32, 33 bottom, 71 top, 84 top right, 99 bottom right; Popsie, New York, 63 top left; Presse-Foto-Gebauer, Bayreuth, 29 top left, middle, and bottom; Pressens Bild, 54 bottom, 62 bottom left, 67 top, 78 top right, 102, 107 top, 111 left and bottom right, 113 left, 115 top

Ras, Barcelona, 74 left; Wilhelm Rauh, Bayreuth, 29 top right; Reportage-bild, 77 middle, 105 top, 122 top left; Björn Rodhe, Göteborg, 108 top, 111 top right; Rodrigues, New York, 73 right; Enar Merkel Rydberg, 13 top, 16 bottom left and right, 17 bottom, 19, 20 top, 74 top right, 76 top right, 77 top, 85 left, 87 bottom left, 90 top, 95 top left, 104 top and bottom right, 114 top left

SAS, 122 bottom left; Eje Sjölander, H.D.-Foto, Helsingbord, 121; Anders Skoog, Bildbyrå Väst, 77 bottom, 118 top left, back jacket photo; Nancy Sorensen, Chicago, 83 top left, 116 right; Donald Southern, London, 90 bottom; Staatsoper, Vienna, 91; Anders Svahn, 115 bottom left, 116 top left, 118 top right and bottom; Svenskt Pressfoto, 105 bottom, 110 top; L. Swięcki, Warsaw, 67 bottom

August Thannhäuser, 20 bottom; Time/Life, New York, 62 top left, 85 right; Felicitas Timpe, Munich, 72 top right; Sabine Toepffer, Munich, 84 left and bottom right, 87 top

United Press International, 50 bottom, 59 top; United States Information Service, 49

Valter Valentin, 12 bottom; Votava, Vienna, 39 top, 112; Alice Vrbsky, New York, 53, 63 bottom left, 64 left, 96

Bengt Wanselius, 122 right; Whitestone Photo, New York, 81 bottom; Alex T. Wilson, London, 76 left

Åhlén & Åkerlunds archiv, 30, 51 right, 108 bottom

From Birgit Nilsson's own collection (photos sent by her admirers and family photos): 8, 9 (bottom right photo by N. K. Torin), 10 (top photo by Harald Wideen), 11 (right photo by Sölling), 14 bottom left, 14 top left on loan from Ingemar Blennow, 15 bottom, 18 bottom right, 22 bottom, 38 bottom, 46, 55 top, 57 bottom left, 58 middle right (Helene Britton), 61, 62 right, 64 top right, 65 bottom left, 68, 69, 70 top left, 72 top left and bottom, 75 middle left and bottom left, 80 top right, 86 bottom middle and bottom right, 98 bottom, 99 bottom left, 107 bottom, 114 top right, 115 bottom right, 116 bottom.